KENYA

By the staff of Editions Berlitz

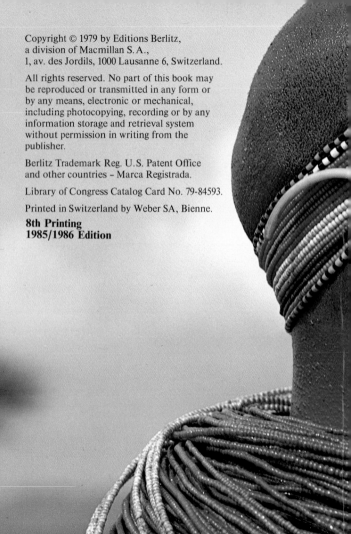

Berlitz Trademark Reg. U.S. Patent Office
and other countries – Marca Registrada.

Library of Congress Catalog Card No. 79-84593.

Printed in Switzerland by Weber SA, Bienne.

8th Printing
1985/1986 Edition

How to use our guide

- All the practical information, hints and tips that you will need before and during the trip start on page 103, with a complete rundown of contents on page 107.

- For general background, see the sections Kenya and the Kenyans, p. 6, and A Brief History, p. 13.

- All the sights to see are listed between pages 28 and 87. Our own choice of sights most highly recommended is pin-pointed by the Berlitz traveller symbol.

- A Who's Who in the Animal World section on pages 39 to 49 fills in on the background to the habits and particularities of the major species you're likely to meet.

- Entertainment, nightlife and all other leisure activities are described between pages 89 and 99, while information on restaurants and cuisine is to be found on pages 100 to 102.

- The Index on page 127 will help you to find what you are looking for.

- Finally, at the back of the book, there's a checklist of animals you might sight.

Although we make every effort to ensure the accuracy of all the information in this book, changes occur incessantly. We cannot therefore take responsibility for facts, prices, addresses and circumstances in general that are constantly subject to alteration. Our guides are updated on a regular basis as we reprint, and we are always grateful to readers who let us know of any errors, changes or serious omissions they come across.

Text: Jack Altman
Photography: Jürg Donatsch
Layout: Doris Haldemann
Illustrations: Aude Aquoise
We wish to thank Ray Morrell and Odhiambo Okite for their contribution to the preparation of this guide. We are also grateful to African Safari Club, the Kenya Tourist Office and T.K. Ngaamba for their valuable assistance.

Cartography: Falk-Verlag, Hamburg.

Contents

Kenya and the Kenyans

The first phenomenon you'll notice in Kenya is the sky, something you might take for granted amidst urban horizons. Here it is quite simply endless and constantly changing in depth and colour. In the heat of the day you'll discover blues, pinks, reds and golds in the light that you never saw before, for Kenya is a feast of colour, light and movement. And in between the stimuli are the most restful beach resorts a tired body could want.

Even on a cloudy day there never seem to be enough clouds to cover the whole sky. You'll watch buffaloes in huge herds making their way across the plateau of the Masai Mara, a few thousand at a time, and the sky will swallow them up. Sitting in a land-rover or minibus, you may suddenly feel very

small, yet somehow at ease to find your proper niche in the scheme of things.

Equally fascinating is the play of colour on every side: the deep red of the soil of Amboseli and Tsavo, the icy white of snow-topped Mount Kenya and the dazzling white of the sandy beaches, the tranquil blue of the ocean and a blue in the lakes that suddenly turns pink when blanketed with a million flamingos, the hot dry green of the savannah and the lusher green of the Aberdare forests.

Movement is similarly diverse. In Nairobi, the pace of the people is an easy-going amble, a swinging gait that reflects the rhythm of the capital's

The vastness of the African skies is a source of perpetual wonder.

business—lively but not frenetic. In the sultry port town of Mombasa the pace is languid; only mad dogs would want it otherwise. Inland to the west, human movement slows to the infinitely patient wanderings of Masai herdsmen, the pace of nomadism itself.

But in the wilds the human being no longer dictates the speed of life. Your eye is taken by the gallop of a herd of zebras, the scamper of an excited troop of baboons or an anxious family of warthogs, the golden flash of a cheetah, the slither of a crocodile in the mud or the slow, purposeful progress of a herd of elephants. This country may be ruled by men and women, but animals are the most honoured tenants.

Kenya is equatorial and thus can offer you the searing heat of Samburu's semi-desert, or the soothing, lukewarm waters of the Indian Ocean; the saturating torpor of Mombasa, but also the heady, bracing air of the cool highlands around Nairobi. Although the capital is less than 150 kilometres from the Equator, you will need a jacket in the evenings at 1,660 metres above sea level. After a day spent in the parched bush of the Masai Mara, you will greet the regular afternoon rains of the Kericho tea plantations as a refreshing respite.

Kenya has emerged as an oasis of calm and stability on a continent that has known little but turmoil in the decades since decolonization. While this has been a great advantage in attracting the tourist trade, it is paradoxically a source of occasional embarrassment. Nairobi is the preferred East African headquarters for news correspondents and is consequently the routine date-line used for reporting wars and political unrest in neighbouring countries. Many inattentive newspaper readers imagine all these disturbances are happening in Nairobi and need to be reassured that Kenya is a safe place for a holiday. The recent peaceful transition of power after the death of President Kenyatta was a source of surprised admiration to some, but Kenyans themselves found it perfectly natural. They attributed the apprehension of outside observers to the contagious effect of reporting power struggles in other African countries.

The Kenyan people have a

Cabbages, coconuts and mangoes —Nairobi market's exotic mix.

9

pronounced taste for the quiet life and a relatively carefree nature that the government is sometimes at pains to stir up into more energetic productivity. But their easy-going character has had the beneficial effect of overcoming the old tensions of tribalism, a major source of conflict elsewhere in Africa. The tribes are formations that rarely go back more than a couple of hundred years and were sustained as elements of colonial administration at a time when they were progressively dissolving and merging into the national unity they are achieving today.

The divisions that Kenyan Africans themselves make in defining their origins are linguistic rather than racial: Bantu-, Nilotic-, Nilo-Hamitic- and Hamitic-speaking peoples. The Kikuyu of the central highlands, part of the Bantu-speaking majority, achieved a dominant position by their direct association with colonial authority after Nairobi was sited on the border of Kikuyu lands. The tribe continues to enjoy considerable prestige and influence despite efforts made by Jomo Kenyatta, the late president and former tribal leader, to dispel ideas that the Kikuyu were in any way superior to other Kenyans.

Daniel arap Moi, member of the minority Nilo-Hamitic Kalenjin tribe, was chosen to succeed Kenyatta in order to combat tribal rivalry between the Kikuyu and the Nilotic-speaking Luo. The Luo, from the shores of Lake Victoria, have developed a reputation as the country's leading intellectuals because of their long connection with European missionary schools, and they fill many of the top university posts.

The most independent of Kenya's tribes is the Masai, a group of tall pastoral nomads who resist the encroachments of modern technological civilization. The Masai guard their herds with spears and still favour the traditional long cloak, though occasionally you may see a young boy wearing a tie-dyed T-shirt.

Kenya's national language is Swahili—Bantu with Arabic influences. This term also refers to the Mohammedan Bantu inhabitants of the coast, distinctive for their mixture of African and Arab features and their pride as merchants with historic ties across the Indian Ocean and Persian Gulf.

Of Kenya's estimated 17,000,000 population, only about 65,000 are of European (mostly British) origin, 200,000

Chadors emphasize beautiful eyes on the predominantly Muslim coast.

are Indian and Pakistani and 42,000 Arab. The European and Indo-Pakistani contingents are what remain of some 60 years of British colonial administration, but the Arab residents go back much further to the settlements founded along the coast from Mombasa up to the island of Lamu in the Middle Ages. The Europeans range from long-established businessmen, hotel managers and farmers to palaeoanthropologists investigating the origins of man and zoologists for whom Kenya is a researcher's paradise. The Indians, Pakistanis and Arabs form distinct commercial classes living in self-contained communities.

The colonial legacy is **11**

marked by the prevalence of the English language, customs and, for want of a better word, cuisine. Vehicles drive on the left. The design of traffic signs, army uniforms and newspapers, the structure of government and public services all show the abiding influence of British models. Even the style of English spoken by African Kenyans reveals colloquialisms from the British colonial and civil services of the 1920s.

But the echoes of the colonial past have been invested with the Kenyans' own casual humour and self-assurance. Conversations about national events of the day are not at all defensive or cautious, as may sometimes be the case in less confident African countries. People have a free-and-easy readiness to criticize shortcomings in authority without at the same time sacrificing an assertive national pride.

When you go to Kenya, be prepared for an exciting sensory experience. You will have a holiday there as you never had before. And come back keener, more alive, more demanding of your usual surroundings.

Don't go out in Malindi's noon sun unless you're born and bred in it.

A Brief History

The first human being to appear in Kenya was perhaps the first human being to appear anywhere. Give or take a few hundred thousand years, he seems to have set up house some 2,500,000 years ago in northern Kenya near the eastern shore of Lake Turkana, or Lake Rudolf as it was known in British colonial times. A fossil of his skull was dug up there in 1972 by a team of palaeo-anthropologists led by Dr. Richard Leakey, the director of the National Museum in Nairobi.

Identified at the National Museum simply as No. 1470, the remains of Kenya's first man predate those found in Java, China and elsewhere in East Africa. Scientists speculate that mankind appeared first in this part of East Africa, rather than anywhere else in the world, because the climate and topographical conditions were appropriate for evolution.

Kenya had changed from a cover of dense rain forest to ever-widening expanses of open savannah. A creature best described as a man-like ape, agile at using trees for his habitat and moving about the ground on all fours, emerged **13** from the forest. In order to look out over the tall savannah grass, to loom larger as a greater apparent threat to predators and to carry food from where it had been gathered or hunted to a safe place for eating, the creature stood up on his hind legs and developed feet for walking and hands for gripping. He became an ape-like man.

The rest, as they say, is history. But it is a history with only the sketchiest of records until the European colonial era. For the rest we must rely on the diggings of palaeoanthropologists and archaeologists.

Stone Age Society

The Stone Age in Kenya seems to have progressed in the classic manner, with fire coming into systematic use around 50,000 B.C. Tools and weapons were progressively refined, particularly with the migration of Caucasoids from south-west Asia and northern Africa. They brought stone arrowheads, knifeblades and ornamental beads made from seeds and discs of ostrich eggshell, dating from around 15,000 B.C.

At this time significant cultural advances took place in the Rift Valley, the great volcanically caused geological fault running through Kenya from Mount Elgon to Mount Kili-

manjaro. In the region between Eldoret and Nairobi, ceremonial burial sites have been found, suggesting the first systematic religious practices. Natural volcanic glass or obsidian was used to make knives that were much longer and more effective than had previously been possible.

By dating rock paintings of long-horned cows found on Mount Elgon and grindstones, pestles, bowls and pots used for grain, it has been estimated that cattle-herding and agriculture emerged only around 1,000 B.C. In fact society in Kenya seems to have remained largely at a Stone Age level until about A.D. 1000, when signs of iron-smelting appeared. Throughout this period there was a constant migration and merging of peoples now identified as Bantu-, Nilotic-, Nilo-Hamitic- or Hamitic-speaking. The gradual change from a hunting-and-gathering society to one of agriculture or pastoralism led to rapid increases in population in the more fertile areas of the highlands and the grazing plateaus of the southwest.

This fellow was perhaps the first human being, found on the banks of Lake Turkana. He's called 1470.

Settlement of the Coast

While the Kenya interior has a written record that goes back only 100 years and sparse information from an oral tradition at most 500 years old, the history of the coastal area begins in Roman times. A Greek merchant living in Roman Egypt made a trip down Africa's east coast to explore trade prospects sometime in the 2nd century A.D. His anonymous account, *The Periplus of the Erythraean Sea* (the Roman name for the Indian Ocean) describes places we know as Lamu, Mombasa and Zanzibar, where the local inhabitants—very tall pirates and seafarers—were ready to trade in ivory, tortoiseshell, rhinoceros horn, coconut oil, gums and spices.

In the next few centuries Arab, Persian, Indian and Chinese merchants arrived on the coast with the help of the Trade Winds. From November to March the north-east monsoon carried them across the ocean to barter for African goods with ceramics, metal hatchets, daggers, lances, glass, wine and wheat. They made the return journey in April, when the south-west monsoon blew their dhows back to the Persian Gulf or India. By the 8th and 9th centuries Arabs began to settle on the north Kenya coast in

what they called the land of the Zenj (the black people). The 10th-century Arab geographer Al-Masudi described the Zenj as a people ruled by elected kings with standing armies and priest-advisors. They used oxen harnessed like horses for transport and for war. They cultivated bananas, millet and coconuts and ate meat and honey.

Trading settlements were established on islands in the Lamu archipelago and spurs of land surrounded by creeks and swamps where their wealth could be easily defended without protective ramparts. The excavated town of Manda in the Lamu archipelago shows an affluent community living in impressive coral-rock houses set with mortar, of a massive construction not found elsewhere in Africa south of the Sahara. In addition to the export of ivory, ambergris, leopard skins, tortoiseshell and gold brought up from what is now Zimbabwe, there are the first records of trade in African slaves, sent to Iraq.

The Shirazi, immigrants from the Persian Gulf, progressively colonized the coast in the 12th century, intermarrying with Africans and developing within two or three generations the mixed Bantu-Arabic language of Swahili, or more pro-

perly, Kiswahili. In trading centres established at Malindi and Mombasa, this Islamic Swahili ruling class kept Africans in a state of slavery, performing menial tasks and tilling the fields. The coastal dwellers thus dealt exclusively with the outside world and had few links to the Kenya interior.

Portuguese Domination
The Portuguese explorer Vasco da Gama arrived on the coast in 1498. The Portuguese, with

Mombasa was always a place worth fighting for, and Fort Jesus was for the Portuguese an almost impregnable stronghold for a hundred years.

commercial centres already established in India, were more interested in setting up new bases for trade across the Indian Ocean than in opening up and colonizing East Africa itself. They were able to make a trading alliance with the Shirazi Sheikh of Malindi, but other city-states, especially Mombasa, resisted Portuguese encroachment.

Mombasa was attacked and plundered by the Portuguese three times in the 16th century—1505, 1528 and 1589—before surrendering its independence. Functioning both as an island-state and a mainland power, with access to military aid from non-Swahili Africans in the hinterland, Mombasa impressed the Portuguese with its great resilience and the material resources it derived from trade with the Middle East and India. In fact it was Mombasa's pre-eminent position that had provoked Malindi's jealousy and pushed it into alliance with the Portuguese.

In the 1580s the Turks, long-time trading partners of Mombasa, sent two expeditions to break the Portuguese blockade of the port. Portuguese retaliation was massive and Mombasa's resistance was overcome by a simultaneous attack in the rear by Zimba warriors who had migrated from the Zambezi valley. Mombasa recovered enough to stage a counter-attack on Malindi, but Malindi's Bantu allies, the Segeja, won a bloody battle, and the town of Mombasa was handed over to the Sheikh of Malindi and the Portuguese in 1592.

Mombasa became the mainstay of Portuguese authority on the coast, placed under the rule of Sheikh Ahmad of Malindi and backed by a Portuguese military garrison in the newly built Fort Jesus. During the next century the whole Swahili coast acknowledged Portuguese supremacy paying customs and tribute to the King of Portugal through his representative, the Captain of Mombasa. But tribute was never paid placidly. The Swahili rulers were encouraged to stage revolts as the Portuguese hold on the coast was gradually weakened by mounting threats to their position elsewhere in the Indian Ocean from the Dutch and British, and from the Persians and Arabs in the Gulf.

After a ferocious assault on Fort Jesus in 1631, the Portuguese were obliged to rule without a sheikh as intermediary. The Imam of Oman supported a major revolt on Pate Island, just north of Lamu, and Fort Jesus was again besieged and plundered in 1660. The Portuguese were finally driven out of Mombasa in 1698. They returned briefly in 1728 but lost their control of the coast for ever the following year.

Having supported Swahili opposition to the Portuguese, Omani Arabs wanted in turn to supplant the Portuguese as the effective rulers of the coastal region. But the Swahilis decided they had had enough of foreign overlords and successfully withstood Omani pressure for over 100 years. Finally Oman's Sayyid Said bin Sultan was able, with political support and second-hand but nonetheless superior naval technology from the British, to establish a foothold on the northern coast with a base at Lamu. In 1837 he was able to conquer Mombasa, but it was felt to be too precarious a place for his seat of power, and he preferred to rule the Eastern African coast from headquarters further to the south in Zanzibar. This Arab supremacy would never have been possible without aid from the region's future rulers, the British.

The Interior in Pre-Colonial Times

During the period prior to British colonization, Kenya's interior was populated—as far as can be ascertained from oral tradition and scanty archaeological findings—by groups that took a long time to achieve the political cohesion of tribal unity. The Nilotic-speaking Luo migrated along the foothills of Mount Elgon from Uganda and Sudan in small family groups, rather than as a tribe—a large group sharing beliefs in a common ethnic identity based on a single mythical founder. They arrived on the shores of Lake Victoria in what is now Nyanza province in the 16th century, but it was not until the late 18th century that they developed a tribal identity, after the change from pastoral to agricultural life and the subsequent fight for land-ownership. Luo tribal unity solidified through the 19th century in wars against neighbouring Nilo-Hamitic tribes of Masai and Nandi. The Masai controlled the grazing lands of south-central Kenya's open plains, while the Nandi held the hill country.

Political organization varied greatly, inevitably clashing later with the uniform system of chieftainships imposed by the British colonial administration. The Bantus of north-western Kenya, for instance, did have a certain centralized organization, with a council of elders advising a clan leader paid for his services in meat, grain or beer. But the eastern Bantu people—most prominently the Kikuyu—occupying the region between Mount Kilimanjaro and Mount Kenya, were organized in peer-groups known as age-sets, each serving a military, police or judicial function in ruling the tribal lands. Solidarity came through kinship and territorial allegiance, rather than loyalty to a central council or chief.

The first Arab contacts with the Kenya interior were cau-

tiously confined to caravans organized from Mombasa, trading cloth, wire, beads and fire-arms in exchange for ivory, mainly from the Kamba tribe. (Unfortunately for Kenya's elephants, the quality of the ivory from their tusks was considered superior to that of Indian elephants and sold better in the Orient.) In the early part of the 19th century attempts at slave-raiding for the thriving Zanzibar trade were quickly abandoned because the Arabs were afraid of risking Masai, Nandi and Kikuyu attacks, which would have jeopardized food and water supplies on the long-distance ivory safaris. The Kikuyu accepted to trade with the Kamba but never allowed the Arab traders into Kikuyu territory.

The caravans opened up routes from Mombasa to Kilimanjaro, and across the Rift Valley, via what is now Nairobi, to Lake Victoria and as far north as Lake Turkana. The Arabs spread the Swahili language along these routes but were never able to gain a hold on the interior itself.

For a Samburu tribesman the fierce wars against European colonizers are just a faint ancestral memory.

Under the Union Jack

In the European partition of Africa in the 1880s, the British colonized Kenya almost as an afterthought. They were mainly interested in strengthening the economic and strategic positions they held in Zanzibar and Uganda. They wanted a means of transport between the coast and the sources of the River Nile. In the first instance this meant building a railway from Mombasa to Lake Victoria. It was only incidentally that they discovered the central highlands through which the railway passed to be good farmland well worth settling. What began as a protected transport corridor was expanded into the full-fledged colony of Kenya.

The first European explorations of the interior were carried out in the 1840s by two Germans, Johann Ludwig Krapf and Johann Rebmann, who worked for the British Church Missionary Society. They located Mounts Kenya and Kilimanjaro, John Hanning Speke discovered Lake Victoria in 1858 and Joseph Thomson explored Masai territory in 1883. (Africans try not to smile patronizingly at European "discovery" of places that they have known about since the beginning of time.) **21**

These men mapped out the territory to be exploited by the Imperial British East Africa Company, set up in 1888. Inept management forced the British government to take over operation of what it called the East African Protectorate seven years later in preparation for the building of the Uganda Railway.

The construction was a legendary struggle against malaria, dysentery, man-eating lions and guerrilla warfare waged by Kamba, Kikuyu and Nandi tribesmen. Some 13,000 Indian coolies formed the backbone of the railway's work force. Hundreds were killed by disease and heat and 28 of them were eaten by lions at Tsavo.

In 1899 the railway reached a well-watered place that had been established during reconnaissance as a staging depot for oxen and mules. It was also the last flat land before the railway would have to make the difficult descent of the Escarpment towards Lake Naivasha. It was decided to make this the new administrative headquarters for the railway and so the town of Nairobi was founded.

When the railway reached Lake Victoria by 1901, Indian traders and European missionaries and settlers had established themselves all along the route—Tsavo, Nairobi, Naivasha, Nakuru and the terminus, Kisumu (Port Florence in those days). The first settlers had come to Kenya in 1896, but official encouragement to people in South Africa, Australia, New Zealand, Canada and Britain began under Commissioner Sir Charles Eliot (1900–04). In 1903 Lord Delamere, a pioneer agriculturalist, was given a grant of 40,000 hectares of rich farmland on the plateau that came to be known as the White Highlands.

When British settlers persuaded the Colonial Office to reserve the White Highlands for them, it was a move not only to exclude the Africans but also the growing number of Indian settlers. Having participated in the construction of the railway and contributed soldiers to the armed force used to crush African resistance, the Indians felt they had a stake in Kenya's future. They had even been encouraged by British commissioners in Uganda and Zanzibar to think of this newly opened territory as a potential "Indian America".

It was in large part to counteract this Indian campaign that the decision was made to shift the capital away from Mombasa, where Oriental traditions were felt to be too strong. Nairobi was made the capital of the Protectorate in 1907, but it was not until 1920 that the region became known as the Crown Colony of Kenya, a name derived from the country's highest peak.

African Ascendency

The British colonial administration interrupted a series of changes taking place among Kenya's tribes by imposing control through a system of tribal chiefs, whom they chose from among men who had led caravans, recruited labour for the railway and new farms or could act as go-between by speaking the growing lingua franca of Swahili. New rivalries developed among ambitious young Africans competing for the wealth and privileges conferred by these chieftainships.

At the same time the British were providing the Africans with weapons for their independence. Christian missionaries gave Africans a European-style education. The revolutionary movements of the 1920s found leaders among graduates of the schools at the Kikuyu Mission Station and the East Africa Scottish Mission at Kibwezi. They were mostly Masai refugees from famine and epidemic, or children of dispossessed landowners from the Highlands. At the Luo Nomia Mission, John Owalo developed a vision of a heaven where he and his African followers, together with Jews and Arabs, would be admitted, while Whites and Indians, he prophesied, would be excluded.

During World War I Kenyan Africans provided several thousand soldiers and over 150,000 military labourers for the campaign in German East Africa. Living and fighting side by side with Europeans, they gained their first direct experience of the white man's real strengths and weaknesses. Veterans of the war returned to lead such militant groups as the Kavirondo Taxpayers and Welfare Association (KTWA) and the Kikuyu Central Association (KCA).

Grievances grew out of the labour recruitment laws. Forced migration moved Africans off their own lands to work in the White Highlands. Herdsmen became farm labourers and fishermen became domestic servants. A policy of "separate development" placed Africans not working European-owned land on "native" reserves, clearly delineated to protect them against illegal encroachment and amended **23**

Indians were among the first foreigners to settle down in Kenya. This frieze in a Swami temple testifies to their pious traditions.

when, in 1931 for instance, gold was found on one of them. Apart from the Swahili towns on the coast, Kenya's urban areas were all European in origin. Africans could work but not live there, except as "sojourners" in shanty towns on the outskirts.

Cutting across tribal lines, the rural KTWA allied Luo with Luyia and the Nairobi-based KCA included both Kikuyu and the Kamba Muslims. Leaders of the movements used their newly acquired education and experience of European ways to combat both colonial practices and the traditional tribal conservatism that kept Africans in submission. An editorial of the KCA newspaper in the 1920s said: "An educated tribe or nation defeats an uneducated tribe or nation. You better swallow that". The writer was a man named Jomo Kenyatta. The British defused the militancy by forcing all grievances to pass through local native councils where the young radical leaders were counterbalanced by moderate elders and British-appointed chiefs under the presidency of the District Commissioner.

The British continued to try to control the drive for independence by courting the moderates among the African leaders. In 1944 Eliud Mathu, educated at Fort Hare University in South Africa and Balliol College, Oxford, was made the first African member of Kenya's Legislative Council. In the same year the colonial administration permitted the formation of a group of African advisors for Mathu, but insisted it be called the "Kenya African Study Union" rather than the too nationalistic-sounding "Kenya African Union". Two years later, Jomo Kenyatta returned to Nairobi after 16 years of study, teaching and political activism in England. He took over Mathu's advisory group, dropped the word "Study" from its title and, as its president from 1947 until it was proscribed in 1952, turned the Kenya African Union from a small educated élite into a mass political movement open to workers, the uneducated and veterans of World War II.

Differences grew between Kenyatta's radicals, who sought independence through revolutionary methods, and the moderates surrounding Mathu, who wanted a gradual, reformist approach. The moderates especially resented Kikuyu domination of the KAU and Kenyatta was agreed that multi-tribal leadership was essential to national independence—a problem that continued to plague him after independence was achieved.

The Mau Mau

The radicals gained the upper hand and events moved relentlessly towards the Mau Mau uprising (the name is believed to have been derived from a Kikuyu warning that the enemy was coming) in 1952, when the Kikuyu led Meru and Embu tribesmen in guerrilla warfare against settlers in the White Highlands. The fighting was fierce. Kenyatta was imprisoned and then exiled to the desert lands of the northern frontier district. Thousands of Kikuyus, Embus and Merus were resettled in guarded areas. Finally in 1956 British troops drove the Mau Mau bands into the Mount Kenya and Aberdare forests, where they were either killed or captured. The casualties of the Emergency, which officially ended in 1960, numbered over 11,000 Mau Mau and close to 2,000 African civilians. Some 50 British troops and 30 European civilians also died.

Armed resistance was broken, but colonial authority was at an end. In 1960 the White Highlands, which cover 800,000 hectares, were opened up to black ownership. British Prime Minister Harold Macmillan spoke of Africa's "winds of change". But Kenya's tribal conflicts were still unresolved as the Kikuyu-dominated Kenya African National Union (KANU) competed for power with the Kenya African Democratic Union (KADU) of the minority tribes. Kenyatta returned from exile to lead the KANU in 1961. Independence was finally achieved on December 12, 1963, and when a republic was proclaimed the next year, Kenyatta was named president.

Independence

The national flag of Kenya is black, red and green—black for the Africans who rule the country, red for the blood shed in the fight for independence and green for the land.

The post-colonial period has been marked by steady Africanization. The land of the old White Highlands has been progressively transferred to African families. An African commercial class has evolved to participate increasingly in previously entirely European- or Asian-owned manufacturing, construction, transportation, tourism and trading businesses. Kenya has developed a mixed economy of private enterprise and state ownership—particularly in banking, petroleum and electricity—as an alternative to the African socialism of neighbouring Tanzania.

Efforts to create an East African Common Market among Kenya, Uganda and Tanzania, particularly through the 1969 Treaty for East African Cooperation, have constantly foundered on the same obstacles that beset the beginnings of the European version: reluctance to relinquish economic sovereignty, imbalances in trade (Tanzania has a chronic trade deficit with Kenya) and recurring political conflicts. Kenya has tried to steer an impartial course, resisting, for example, Tanzanian pressures to close off Uganda's trade access to the Indian Ocean through Mombasa.

Mzee (Honourable Old Man), as Kenyatta was known, exerted a unifying and charismatic leadership through the 15 years of his presidency. His international prestige, even among his old British enemies, greatly boosted Kenyan self-confidence. His successors have a solid foundation to build on.

Modern times have not yet brought industrial air pollution. Clothes hung out to dry won't come in dirty.

What to See

Nairobi

It's a good idea to spend at least a couple of days in Nairobi before heading for the coast or the game reserves. You'll understand why Kenya has been so successful in making the transition from colony to stable republic. It's important to remember that Nairobi was never conceived as an African town; it was artificially created as a convenient place for railway builders and then colonial administrators. For most of the colonial era Africans weren't even allowed to live there. Now you'll see a city whose European beginnings are gradually being Africanized while drawing on modern European and American technology.

Nairobi is the largest of the East African cities, with a population currently estimated at one million. In a country where hurry is nowhere considered a virtue, the central streets of Nairobi almost bustle. What makes this even conceivable so close to the Equator is the mile-high town's delightfully temperate climate, which greatly influenced the British in their choice of a capital for their colony.

But in 1899 when construction first began, Nairobi was described as "a bleak, swampy stretch of soggy landscape, devoid of human habitation of any sort". The Masai were more complimentary, calling the area *Nakusontelon* (The Beginning of All Beauty). Certainly the climate has since borne out the Masai rather than the railway builders, making it possible for Nairobi to boast the name "City of Flowers" with abundant hibiscus, jacaranda, bougainvillea, frangipani and acacia along highways and roundabouts and in lush parks and gardens.

In 1902 the place was nearly abandoned when plague swept the town, which was burned to the ground at the recommendation of a doctor. "Town" was a big word for it—a few rows of tents, barracks slapped together out of corrugated iron, some Indian shops, a soda-water factory, railway yards and one ramshackle hotel called Wood's. It was a frontier town, in fact.

Despite another plague in 1904, Nairobi was rebuilt and by the time the Protectorate had officially established its headquarters there in 1907 the great white hunters were

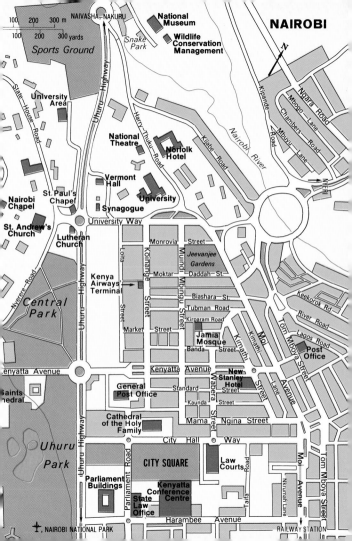

streaming in to start off on safari from the Norfolk Hotel. The most prominent of them was Theodore Roosevelt, the United States president, who headed a safari with 500 porters, all dressed in blue and each carrying 25 kilos of supplies. In ten months—while out of office—Roosevelt bagged 296 animals.

But it was not till the 1930s that Nairobi began to emerge from its primitive frontier beginnings to look something like the city of today, which covers 650 square kilometres, including the airport and the Nairobi National Park. Because it is hemmed into a triangle by the Nairobi River on the north, the railway on the south and the six-lane Uhuru Highway on the west, the central area is developing skyward with high-rise buildings rather than expanding outwards.

The building that dominates the skyline, the huge **Kenyatta Conference Centre,** neatly symbolizes the interaction of Nairobi's European origins and African destiny by combining a cylindrical skyscraper that would not be out of place in London, Brussels or Frankfurt with a cone-shaped congress hall reminiscent of tribal African thatched structures. The Conference Centre, completed in 1973, has a revolving restaurant on top of a tower, which merits a trip at least for the view of the city and the surrounding hills. It is found in City Square along with the old—to the extent that anything in Nairobi is old—neo-Classical Law Courts, the very model of an English county court building, and other administrative offices.

White-columned arcades, the dominant feature of architecture in the business district, are perfectly adapted to the climate, protecting you from the sudden rains or midday sun as you make your way around town. These typical arcades shelter the shops and restaurants along Mama Ngina Street—formerly Queensway and now named after Kenyatta's wife—and Kimathi Street, named after Dedan Kimathi, a Mau Mau leader executed by the British in 1957. Kenyatta Avenue is the broadest of the central streets; it was constructed in pioneer days to enable 12-span oxcarts to wheel around without difficulty.

Jomo Kenyatta's Conference Centre towers over Nairobi's skyline just as he dominates Kenya's history.

Two of the great traditional meeting-places of Nairobi are the Norfolk and New Stanley Hotels, which you can enjoy even if you are staying elsewhere. The **Norfolk,** in Harry Thuku Road—damaged in a fire in early 1981—is only eight years younger than Nairobi itself. Have tea on the Delamere terrace or a gin and tonic in the bar with its caricatures of old colonial types on the walls and you'll catch a whiff of the decades when the lion, the symbol of Kenya, had a Union Jack on its tail.

The **New Stanley's** claim to fame is its Thorn Tree, a café in Kimathi Street. Hunters and other travellers would leave messages pinned to the trunk of a huge acacia with yellow bark rising from the middle of the café and the tradition remains, although the hunters have been replaced by tourists and the old acacia has been replaced by a new one: Franz tells Heidi (and the rest of us) that he'll meet her in Cairo, and Debbie tells Billy Joe she won't be able to join him in Marrakesh.

Nairobi is quite ecumenical in its religious buildings. The Jamia Mosque was built in 1933 by the Sunni sect of Islam on the Kirparam Road, north of Kenyatta Avenue. Mass is said in Swahili and hymns are sung in traditional African rhythms at the modern Cathedral of the Holy Family on City Hall Way. The Anglican All Saints Cathedral, west of Uhuru Park, is the epitome of English ecclesiastical architecture. There is also a synagogue, west of the University of Nairobi.

The **National Museum,** on Museum Hill at the northern end of Uhuru Highway, deserves a visit above all for its prehistoric collection, depicting the origins of man and various animals. On exhibit here is No. 1470, the skull of our two-and-a-half million-year-old ancestor discovered at Lake Turkana (see p. 13). There are also the findings from Olduvai Gorge in Tanzania: fossilized remains, perhaps 1,650,000 years old, of *homo habilis,* the first tool-making man, with his stone hand-axes and cleavers; and *homo erectus,* a 1,150,000-year-old man coming closer to the brain capacity of *homo sapiens.*

The remains of prehistoric animals include a giant ostrich, a rhinoceros that makes his present-day descendant look like a rabbit, and a two-million-year-old fossilized elephant, which could be brought into the museum only by knocking down one of the walls. In the museum courtyard is the stuffed version of a modern-day monster: Ahmed, the legendary elephant from Marsabit, with huge tusks, who was declared a national monument by President Kenyatta after two American hunters threatened to shoot the beast. Ahmed died a natural death in 1974, aged about 60. On a smaller scale are the magnificent bird, insect and butterfly collections—the latter protected from moths by camphor balls.

Opposite the National Museum is the **Snake Park,** where you can see snakes, crocodiles, lizards and other examples of Kenya's reptile life. For those who like that kind of thing, you can watch the snakes being "milked" for their venom, usually on Wednesday afternoons.

If you are visiting Nairobi before you set off for the national parks and game reserves, you may want to tour the **Nairobi National Park.** Established in 1945, this was the first national park to be created in Kenya. It has a beautifully varied landscape of forest, hills and savannah; but if you've already visited other parks, Nairobi's well-marked, smooth-surfaced roads may seem a little too tame and civilized in comparison to, say, Samburu or Masai Mara.

Otherwise Nairobi makes a good introduction.

There are lots of lions, and the gate keepers at the park entrance may tell you where they are to be found each day. Also look out for the ostriches (who do *not* bury their heads in the sand), baboons, zebras, giraffes, warthogs, and elands—antelopes whose tasty meat and milk have attracted the interest of animal breeders hoping to develop herds on special farms. Although the animals are fenced off on one side of the park from the Nairobi–Mombasa highway, they have free access for migration to and from Amboseli and Tsavo across the Athi and Kaputei Plains. If you have missed some of the animals at the other parks and reserves because they were too shy, you will find them so blasé about vehicles here they'll practically pose full-face, profile or rear view as requested. One of the great advantages of Nairobi National Park is for the photographer.

At the western end of the park is the **Animal Orphanage,** founded in 1963, mostly with donations collected by Dutch schoolchildren to provide a home for young animals deserted in the wild by their parents and unable to survive alone. Zoologists who care for

The neo-Classical architecture of Nairobi's Law Courts is a strong reminder of the country's British colonial past, set against a solid background of modern progress. All of which can be said with flowers.

them until they are able to be returned to the reserves have a chance to study these animals up close and children can take their first easy look at Kenya's animal riches. But for the rest of us, with the abundance of wide-open parks and reserves so easily available, the orphan-age is little more than a glorified zoo and has a limited appeal.

If your appetite for prehistoric remains has been whetted by the National Museum, you might be tempted to make an excursion to **Olorgesailie,** 40 miles west of Nairobi. A national park has been declared to protect the Stone Age camp-

site excavated in the 1940s by Louis and Mary Leakey, the famous palaeoanthropologists whose son is now director of the Nairobi Museum. In thatched-roof shelters is an excellent collection of the tools and weapons that were found lying about the ground, exposed to the elements but miraculously preserved. Among the implements discovered are what seem to be early versions of Argentinian *bolas*, stones grouped in threes, strung together and thrown at the legs of running animals to trip them up.

The ride down to Olorgesailie is also an expedition to the bed of the **Rift Valley,** and you will see a lot of that awe-inspiring phenomenon as you make your way to the game reserves. To obtain an overall view of the immensity of the valley, try to make at least one journey between the national parks and the capital by small aircraft.

National Parks and Game Reserves

Every nation has its monuments and Kenya's are not cathedrals, palaces or museums, but rather the wildlife that roams the length and breadth of the country. Animals and birds are accorded a privileged position in the life of Kenya and are protected against the wanton hunting and poaching that have nearly decimated many species. For instance, the elephant population dropped from 165,000 in 1970 to at most 60,000 by 1978. Leopards, between 2,000 and 5,000 in 1971, are now seldom seen.

As the human population has grown, urban areas and farmland have expanded and a system of national parks and game reserves (operated by local authorities) has been developed to protect humans from the wild animals and vice versa.

This system has enabled the wildlife to survive in its natural habitat—though the old migration patterns have necessarily been somewhat modified and ecologists are studying what long-range effect this might have. It has also provided tourists with the perfect opportunity to view the animals going about their normal business of hunting, eating, drinking and mating.

Safaris (a Swahili word meaning simply "journey") are organized into the bush in jeeps and minibuses with adjustable roofs to see the wildlife at close quarters. It is quite exhilarating to wake at dawn and have a quick cup of coffee or tea with the sunrise and then go on a game-run at the best time for viewing animals on the move, before they settle down to rest in the heat of the day. And you return to your lodge or campsite for a proper English-style breakfast.

You will have many opportunities for photographing, filming and simple viewing with binoculars. But it's important to remember as you read or hear about what animals you can expect to see at this or that park, that they're not always to be found in the same place; they migrate, weather conditions change and availability of food and water varies from day to day. With so much arranged for you, don't be too upset if some animals don't choose to conform to the tour organizers' plans. A guide to some of the "monuments" of Kenya with their Swahili names begins on p. 39.

Dos and Don'ts in the National Parks and Game Reserves

You soon learn to accept the rules and restrictions operating in the parks and reserves as more than reasonable in the interest of preserving both the wildlife and the natural beauty around you.

National parks exclude all human residence except hotels, lodges and specially designated campsites, while game reserves permit only a limited number of herdsmen with their cattle. No other creatures, including your pet dog, are allowed to enter these areas.

Touring the parks and reserves is permitted only during daylight hours—roughly from 6 a.m. to an elastic 6 p.m. You very quickly get into a rhythm of early rising and early nights to take maximum advantage of the chances to see wildlife up close. There is plenty to be seen throughout the day, but it is a good idea to take a siesta in preparation for one last run before dusk. This is when the carnivores begin their hunt for dinner, and it's the only time of day when the more elusive animals come out of hiding.

For their own safety and to avoid disturbing the animals, tourists are confined to their vehicles during a safari, except at special signposted sites where it is permitted to walk about. This may at times be frustrating but it has a certain humbling effect on human beings, who for once are caged in while the animals roam free in their natural habitat.

Driving speeds are usually limited to 48 kilometres per hour inside the parks, but it is best to drive even slower than that. You will see more, disturb the animals less and stir up less dust. It is a deliberate government policy not to tarmac the park roads, which are uneven and often potholed so as to force traffic to slow down and to keep the parks in their natural state.

The Ministry of Tourism and Wildlife will assign rangers to accompany you on game-runs and it is highly recommended that you make use of this service. The rangers are usually local residents who know the game country inside out and can guide you to the places most likely to shelter the more elusive animals, as well as provide information and folklore about the animals' habits.

In some parks you are allowed to leave the roads and go across open country—make sure you have a sturdy four-wheel-drive vehicle—but it is advisable not to do this without a ranger. Be sure to take a little food and drink in case your car breaks down.

Who's Who in the Animal World

Elephant *(Tembo or Ndovu).* Although the lion has long been regarded as the king of beasts, when you see animals working out their own hierarchy in nature, you are likely to conclude that the real supreme monarch is the elephant. Certainly the lion himself makes way. You cannot fail to be impressed, even awed, by the prodigious nobility of elephants as they wander around in search of fresh grass, leaves or juicy bark, a cool water-hole or some mud to wallow in. You may also see them blowing dust over themselves with their trunks, then rubbing themselves against trees to remove ticks.

An adult male, three metres tall, often weighs around 5,400 kilos and each tusk may weigh up to 90 kilos. The female, just under three metres, weighs a mere 2,700 kilos. But the females do all the work and are the leaders of herds that group their own baby and

There's something about an elephant that inspires respect. It's a matter of unquestionable dignity.

adolescent offspring and that of their daughters. Male elephants are chased away from the herd as soon as they are old enough to fend for themselves, at around 12 to 14 years, and join up with other males.

Enormously affectionate mothers, the females also do all the fighting to protect their young from lions and hyenas. The males turn up only when one of the females goes into heat. Pregnancy lasts up to 22 months, the longest of any mammal. Living till about 50–60 years, elephants are known to bury their own dead and indeed other dead animals, even dead humans they have killed; but, contrary to legend, they do not have mass burial grounds. (When elephant skeletons have been found en masse, it has invariably been due to mass killings carried out by humans encircling an elephant herd with fires.)

Lion *(Simba).* It may be arguable whether the lion is the king of the jungle, but nobody would dispute that this is the most feared of African predators. Lions are ferocious hunters, but in the daylight hours when you will see them, they are more likely to seem docile, lazy and imperturbable and downright friendly. Unless, of course, they were unable to find a meal during the night, in which case their hunger might rouse them to action.

Lion prides, comprising several small families spread over a wide area, are more loosely knit groups than elephant herds. Lions roam over a territory that covers perhaps 50 square kilometres in threes and fours, usually lionesses with their cubs, while male lions roam together, keeping separate from the females until mealtime.

With an arrogance that would enrage the mildest feminist, the male leaves almost all the hunting to the female and just waits for the kill, at which point, weighing up to 180 kilos compared with the 110-kilo female, he moves in, fights off the lioness and her cubs and takes—the lion's share. But it should be said in the male's defence that his presence as a sentinel does keep the pride area safe for the lioness and her cubs.

The lion's favourite prey is zebra and buffalo. Both are big enough for a hearty meal for the whole family but also strong enough, especially the buffalo, to require group effort to make the kill. Most antelopes can be knocked off single-handed.

Lions are very sensuous beasts and like to lick, groom and rub up against each other, often as an act of group solidarity before the hunt or just out of good fellowship during the after-dinner siesta. Males are especially vain about grooming their opulent mane, their chief sexual selling-point. The roar, heard most often before dawn or early evening, is a crescendo of deep rolling grunts quite unlike that fabricated MGM groan.

Baboon *(Nyani).* Behaviourists have used the *baboon* as an analogy for theorizing about natural aggressiveness and male dominance among human beings. Quite apart from the dubious value of making such parallels, recent observations of baboons have shown them to be motivated not by fear and brutal tyranny, as had been claimed, but by strong family relationships and social co-operation.

While the males play an important role in guaranteeing the safety of the baboon troop, it is the females who provide the troop's stability. Females stay in the troop all their lives, while males are constantly on the move. Social cohesion is built around the family, with perhaps as many as 20 related units of mother and offspring.

The males form a separate band moving on the outskirts of the troop as it hunts for food.

You will frequently see male, female and baby baboons grooming each other. Their communal search for ticks, knots and dirt is an activity which reinforces group solidarity and what zoologists do not hesitate to call friendship. Male and female baboons form companionships independent of sexual mating. There is a hierarchy of prestige among female baboons, and the males seek a reflected glory by associating with prominent females, who are the troop's effective leaders and decide when it is time to move and which direction to take.

Baboons will eat young shoots of savanna grass, shrubs and herbs, but their favourite food is fruit, especially figs. They also occasionally turn carnivore and hunt down birds, hare and young gazelles. Nothing would be safe on an unguarded picnic. Baboons, ever playful, are frequently naughty, even vicious when provoked, but a long way from being obnoxious criminals.

Giraffe *(Twiga).* In 1414 the Chinese Emperor was sent a unicorn as a gift through Arab traders in Malindi; but when it turned out to be a giraffe he was reportedly not disappointed. Giraffes are the best argument for seeing animals in Kenya in their natural habitat, rather than in a zoo. You may think you already know what this weird beast looks like, but a delightful surprise awaits you when you finally spot one towering over the plain or decorously moving out between the trees on a hillside.

The giraffe seems to have achieved a state of grace, an ineffable dignity, just from being quite literally above it all—as much as 5 metres for males. He relies on acute eyesight and his privileged vantage point to see potential dangers long before they arrive, fleeing instead of coping with them in a fight. He gets his liquid from juicy or dew-covered foliage, so as not to have to bend down too often to drink ground water in an ungainly split vulnerable to attack from lions.

Females give birth standing up and the calf, already almost two metres tall and weighing 65 kilos, is dropped over a metre to the ground, head first and with a considerable thud. The fall

Next page: *You might catch the attention of a hyena, giraffe or lion. Baboons prefer nit-picking.* **41**

breaks the umbilical cord. Freud would not be surprised to learn that this rude arrival on earth prepares the calf for a not very affectionate upbringing from the aloof female giraffe.

Hyena *(Fisi).* You're not supposed to like hyenas. With their oversized heads, sloped backs, scruffy fur and clumsy gait, they're ugly. They have a dozen ways to make a horrible din, including a whoop, a groan, a low giggle, yell, growl, whine and the famous blood-curdling laugh. And they have a miserable reputation as cowardly scavengers, waiting for other predators to do their hunting for them and feeding off the remains.

But field studies have revealed hyenas to resort much more to hunting than scavenging for their food. They hunt with considerable intelligence and courage, even attacking rhinoceros and young elephants. In fact, precisely because lions are stronger than hyenas, they can always steal the latter's kill and actually rely more on scavenging than the much maligned hyenas. So much for reputations.

Grouped in closely knit clans of up to 20 members, they live in a den with entrance holes connected by a network of tunnels. They mark out the clan territory with their dung and go on regular border patrols to keep out rival clans. Unusual among the mammals, the females are stronger and heavier than the males (58 as against 54 kilos). This evolution is thought to result from the mother's need to protect her young against the male hyena's frequent cannibalistic tendencies.

Clan solidarity is constantly reinforced, particularly before a hunt, with elaborate meeting-ceremonies: hyenas sniff each other's mouths, necks and heads, raise a hind leg and lick each other before going off, reassured, on the group activity. Hunting is carefully co-ordinated. Typically, hyenas will start to chase a herd of wildebeests (gnus) and suddenly stop again to take stock of the herd in motion. One of them spots a weakling and the chase resumes. They bring down the chosen victim with a series of well-aimed bites and the end is swift.

Rhinoceros *(Kifaru).* There is a certain sad poetry in the thought that the huge, lumbering, ill-tempered rhinoceros has a horn which in powdered form is believed in the Orient to be an aphrodisiac. The historic and highly profitable quest for his horn has aggravated the poor rhino's temper. Other animals on the game reserves have grown used to human beings, but every time a rhino sees us —and his tiny eyes don't see very well—he assumes we're after his blessed horn again.

Rhinos in Kenya have dwindled from 8,000 in the 1960s to about a thousand now. Although they may move around in twos and threes, they are more often seen alone. There is nothing more desolate than the screaming groan of a solitary rhino disturbed by another at his water-hole.

The one creature that can approach the rhino with impunity is the oxpecker (or tick bird) which perches on the rhino's back. In exchange for the rhino's ticks and flies, the oxpecker provides a loudly chattering alarm system to warn the sleeping rhino of any approaching danger.

Mother rhinos are ferocious defenders of their young. A concerted attack by three male lions on a rhino calf resulted in one of the lions being killed and the other two slinking away. The rhino can move his 1,350-kilo bulk up to 55 kilometres per hour, at least as fast as a lion, with amazing ability to wheel suddenly to face an attack from the rear.

There's nothing delicate about rhinos, not even their love making, which is accompanied by a lot of ferocious snorting and jousting resistance from the female before she finally submits. Unlike the few seconds expended by most animals, copulation between rhinos lasts more than 30 minutes and this is thought to account for the mythic properties attributed to that horn.

Zebra *(Punda Milia)*. The big question is not how the zebra got his stripes, but why he bothered in the first place. The stripes don't act as effective camouflage nor are they a means of sexual attraction, since males and females have essentially the same coats— with sub-species ranging in colour from black and white to brown and beige. The best guess so far is that the subtle individual variations of zebras' stripes enable them to recognize each other at a distance. Whatever the explanation, the optical effect of a couple of hundred zebras at full gallop can make your head spin.

The herd consists of strong family units, in which a stallion

On following page: *A cheetah can be distinguished from a leopard by his smaller head. Zebras, rhino.* **45**

Fritz Bucher, Zürich

stays together with up to six mares and their foals, and groups of male bachelors. The bachelor groups are quite frivolous, like American college fraternities, spending most of their time racing, wrestling and generally fooling around. Relations between the stallion and his "harem" are cordial, enhanced by mutual grooming. If you have a nice striped coat, you keep it in good shape. Unlike many animals, the zebra stallion does not seem to fear being cuckolded and is friendly and courteous to other stallions.

When lions or hyenas threaten, the stallion stands his ground, biting and kicking them to give his family time to escape. This ploy is often successful because lions prefer to rely on surprise attack, rather than a pitched battle, for making their kill and hyenas much prefer to tackle a weakling, rather than a stallion.

Cheetah *(Duma)*. How do you tell a cheetah from a leopard? First, his body markings are round spots with pronounced black "tear-marks" on the face, whereas the leopard's spots are like groups of five fingerprints and the face is spotted rather than "tear-marked". More importantly, if you get the chance to watch them, you will see the cheetah is much more lithe and elegant, and taller and slimmer than the leopard. If you want to compare the leopard to a handsome woman, then the cheetah is a superb mannequin with the same cool aloofness.

Cheetahs are not very gregarious, often hunting alone and so unable to protect their kill when attacked by scavenging lions, hyenas or even vultures. A mother will dutifully rear her cubs and then part abruptly from them. They never acknowledge each other again. Male cheetahs fend for themselves, occasionally hunting with a couple of other males, and meeting up with females only for mating and then only after a fierce fight.

The mother's training of her cubs for hunting is a careful affair, as befits the fastest mammal on earth, 112 kilometres per hour compared with the fastest racehorse's 77 k.p.h. At first the mother cheetah makes the kill herself, usually by biting through the prey's windpipe. The cub picks up the dead prey by the throat and "strangles" it again. Gradually the mother lets the growing cub have first go at catching the prey and only if he botches it will she intervene so as not to risk losing the meal altogether.

Closed Season

The Kenyan government declared a total ban on hunting in May 1977, in an attempt to restore ecological balances after years of wholesale killing threatened many species with extinction. The sale of trophies is also outlawed.

Government officials do not want to commit themselves on when hunting might be restored, but it would be only on the strictest quota system for a few animals reaching ecologically excessive numbers.

Or else the mother makes the first thrust and then leaves the weakened prey for the cub to finish off. By about the age of 14 months the cub is ready to do the job alone. Mother can go. You have a fair chance of witnessing some of this, as the cheetah is the only big cat to hunt by day, mostly in the early morning.

Leopard *(Chui)*. Leopards are always described as elusive and you will indeed be lucky to see one unless you are in one of those game lodges that lures leopards to floodlit platforms with bait. They keep to the cover of trees and dense undergrowth and their solitary, stealthy habits are enabling them to survive poachers much better than lions and cheetahs.

While females seem to roam at will, male leopards are definitely territorial, staking out their home ranges by spraying urine along the boundaries and fighting off other males who might trespass. A leopard's usual roar sounds like wood sawing, but during mating there's a snarling and caterwauling reminiscent of alley cats, only ten times louder. The females make affectionate mothers and, unlike cheetahs, continue to meet with their offspring after they've grown up and left home.

Leopards are nocturnal beasts, spending the day resting in the shade, either under an overhanging hillside rock or up a tree, anywhere where they can survey the surrounding countryside. Weighing between 35 and 55 kilos on an average, they are very powerful and versatile hunters, prepared to kill anything from small birds to animals three times their size. Leopards can carry 45 kilos of uneaten meat up into the higher branches of a tree out of the reach of scavengers. They particularly like eating other carnivores such as foxes, jackals and serval cats, which accounts for their notorious partiality for domestic dogs on occasions when they have wandered into town.

49

Aberdare and Mount Kenya

Aberdare* National Park, north of Nairobi and west of Mount Kenya, is a good place to begin sightseeing. Animals here don't have to run fast to get away from predators—or human beings—because they have the protection of concealment in dense rain forest and bamboo jungle. Consequently, since it is not easy to catch sight of them when you are driving around the park, several hotels have been built as viewing-posts. They are perched high on stilts in the middle of the forest, usually near a water-hole.

The pioneer of these is **Treetops,** on the eastern edge of the park. It was originally built in 1932, a single cabin for a few guests who would go there on moonlit nights to see the wild animals wander over to the water-hole and natural salt-lick (soil covered with natural deposits of sodium chloride). By

---

* Aberdare is the old colonial name, after the Victorian President of the Royal Geographical Society. The Kikuyu name, Nyandarua, is gradually replacing it but hasn't quite caught on yet.

With Mount Kenya in the background, waterbucks drink before the elephants and buffaloes arrive.

50

Bruce Coleman Ltd, Uxbridge

1952 its popularity had grown and it was expanded and spruced up to receive an illustrious young couple, Princess Elizabeth and the Duke of Edinburgh. (The night of their stay, news came of the death of King George VI and Princess Elizabeth's accession to the English throne.)

An "artificial moon" was installed—floodlighting—and a little extra salt was added to the lick to keep the animals happy. However disturbing they might be to the sensibilities of nature-loving purists, the artifices of floodlighting and extra salt don't seem to upset the animals themselves. Why shouldn't the moon shine every night? Wild dogs have not been observed to go wilder; they apparently know the real thing.

The Aberdare forest provided natural cover for the Mau Mau when British armed forces mounted their counter-attack in the 1950s. In 1954 the Mau Mau burned down Treetops—not a difficult operation as it was, and is again, made entirely of wood. It was rebuilt three years later.

Because of the proximity of the wild animals, you and the other guests will be asked to meet in the nearby town of NYERI (at the Outspan Hotel, built around the old home of Robert Baden-Powell, founder of the Boy Scouts) to be driven in minibuses to the edge of the forest. There a guide armed with a rifle will usher you cautiously on foot to the hotel. You'll be warned to keep together and be quiet so as not to disturb the odd—and lethal—buffalo that might be in the neighbourhood. The path to the hotel is dotted with little timbered enclosures in which you can take cover if surprised by a wild visitor.

At the hotel you will be served tea and cakes, which you may have to share with the baboons and hornbills who find this hotel-on-stilts formula an excellent supplement to their diet. For the rest of the evening and after dinner as late into the night as you care to stay awake, you can settle down to a marvellous parade of elephants, rhinos, antelopes and buffaloes. Watching them congregate around the waterhole, you can observe how they accept their hierarchy. The antelope makes way for the buffalo, who steps aside for the rhino, and they all move out of the way for the elephant. However late you may have stayed up, it is worth getting up at dawn to see the sun rise over the snowy peaks of Mount Kenya.

The Ark, closer to the Aberdare mountain range and accessible via the Aberdare Country Club, has the same formula as Treetops, but on a more luxurious scale. As its name suggests, it is built—again on stilts— in the form of Noah's ark, with a gangplank leading you over the trees to the entrance. There is a "dungeon" in the basement to give you an elephant's eye-view of the animals. If you are lucky, you may catch a glimpse of the rare *black* leopard or smaller *black* serval cat. This rarity is due to the high altitude—over 2,500 metres—which is thought to cause melanism, a blackening of the animals' coats.

In **Mount Kenya's** forest-covered foothills, which also constitute a national park, is another hotel-on-stilts: **Mountain Lodge,** at the southwest edge of the mountain, is accessible by car. (For all these places you must book ahead.) Mountain Lodge brings you right to the heart of the rain forest, compared with Treetops, where the elephants' destruction of the trees has greatly expanded the clearing around the water-hole. There is even a "game-watchman" who will wake you up if one of the animals you have "asked for" appears at the water-hole.

Here you are plunged into a clamour of sounds and the heady smells of primeval forest, the Africa you dreamed of.

But the chief attraction of the region is Mount Kenya. The snow-covered peaks of Africa's second highest mountain are right on the Equator. When the German missionary-explorer Johann Ludwig Krapf reported this fact to Europe in 1849, he was laughed at. It was not until Joseph Thomson, a Scotsman, confirmed his observation 34 years later that the equatorial snow was accepted as fact.

There are three peaks— Batian (5,199 metres), Nelion (5,188 metres) and Lenana (4,985 metres)—all lava "plugs" that thrust through volcanic eruptions when the mountain was 1,800 metres higher ten million years ago. The two highest peaks are regularly scaled by experienced climbers, while the Lenana is a relatively easy climb and has become known as "Tourist Peak".

The origin of the mountain's name is disputed and has developed into a matter of tribal pride, since it became the name of the country. The Masai call it *Erukenya* (Misty Mountain), which is romantically true for nine months of the year. The Kikuyu call it *Kirinyaga* (White and Glorious Mountain) and

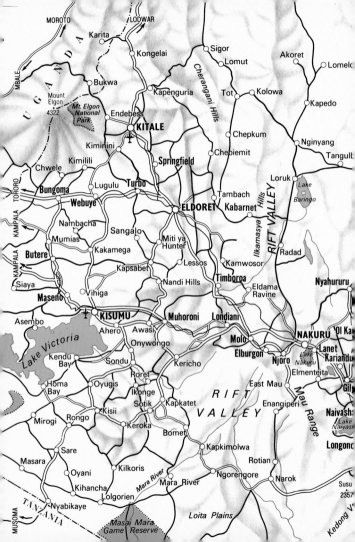

the Kamba call it *Kya Nyaa* (Hill of the Cock Ostrich).

If you have the time and a good pair of lungs, it's well worth attempting the Lenana climb at least. After being cooped up in a vehicle during most of your day-time safaris, you'll enjoy the chance to walk through dense forest changing to bamboo jungle at 2,500 metres and then, at 3,000 metres, to clearings surrounded by charming Abyssinian Hagenia trees (the fruit of which is a fine antidote to stomach-worms) hung with orchids, old-man's beard and other creepers. The walk is a botanist's delight and experiences like this change steel-and-concrete city dwellers, who never thought of "nature" as being anything but cats, dogs, pigeons and dandelions, into amateur zoologists, ornithologists or botanists overnight (see p. 92).

The climb is not likely to be dangerous. The animal you will see most frequently is the little hyrax, sometimes called a rock-rabbit. However, it has hoofs rather than paws and this, plus its digestive system,

Hotels on stilts, a speciality of Kenya's animal-watching, are made from the wood of the rain forests.

relates it, believe it or not, to the elephant.

Three jet-setters got together in 1958 to convert the Mawingo Hotel in NANYUKI to a deluxe complex, the **Mount Kenya Safari Club.** In a superb 100-acre landscaped garden, there's everything from airstrips to bird observation towers, from swimming pools to restaurants to entertain you—lavishly.

Samburu

The Samburu-Buffalo Springs Game Reserve, on the River Uaso Nyiro north of Aberdare, is small by Kenyan standards. You'll have excellent opportunities to see a wide variety of game in a compact area of 330 square kilometres.

At the **Samburu Game Lodge,** a well-equipped hotel beside the river, you can go down to the Crocodile Bar at the water's edge and sip an evening aperitif with a ringside view of crocodiles having their supper (thoughtfully served on the river bank by the hotel kitchens). The lodge lures leopards out of the dense forest with meat on a floodlit platform. It's a very rare treat indeed when this Greta Garbo of the animal kingdom deigns to make an appearance. Most often the bait is gobbled up by little genet cats or white-tailed **57**

A photo safari on the game reserve caters to every need and comfort. Camps have tented dining rooms.

mongooses—a less spectacular act, perhaps, than the star performance the public is waiting for, but endearing nonetheless.

On the early morning game-run you will be able to criss-cross the reserve in search of lions or rhinoceros—this is one of the reserves where the country is flat enough for your vehicle to leave the regular roads. In your search for the hunters' famous Big Five—lions, leopards, elephants, buffaloes and **58** rhinos—your best bet is to stay

close to the river, especially in the dry season. But be sure you don't miss Samburu's special attractions: the reticulated giraffe, treasured for his bronze, web-patterned coat as the most handsome of the species and found only here and, less visibly, at Meru and Marsabit reserves; and the equally scarce Grevy's zebra, with trumpet-shaped ears and a coat more intricately striped than that of the common variety.

If you want to avoid hotel life, there is a campsite where tents can be rented in BUFFALO SPRINGS, south of the river. There are also several other tented campsites, both

on the bank of the Uaso Nyiro and to the south-east along Champagne Ridge, where you'll have a good view across the reserve. Camping is particularly recommended for bird-watchers, for whom Samburu provides a bewildering variety. One expert has spotted 363 species, including the African hawk eagle, the buff-crested bustard, the Egyptian goose and the lilac-breasted roller; but even a complete amateur will grow to know and love the schoolmasterly hornbill, the idiotic guinea fowl and, everybody's favourite, the vulture, nature's most efficient garbage collector. One of the good things about vultures is that if you see them clustered in the trees somewhere, they act as a good signpost to one of the big cats sitting by the remains of his prey—while the vultures wait their turn.

Lakes Nakuru and Naivasha

After the restrictions, however necessary, of the big game parks it makes a pleasant change to visit the tranquil lakes of Nakuru and Naivasha, south-west of Samburu, and walk in broad daylight without worrying about being eaten alive. A variety of birds are **59** attracted to the area, with several hundred species counted at each lake.

Lake Nakuru is considered by leading ornithologists to be quite simply the finest in the world for sighting birds. But even if that doesn't impress you, the sight of a million or more—in exceptional years *two* million—pink flamingos in a wide band along its shoreline should. And then there are hundreds of other species to be seen, if you care to persevere. The lake is surrounded by a national park, where you'll be in the company of docile waterbuck, impala and baboons galore. The park extends to the foothills of the Mau Range, in which rhinos roam around as well as a few lions and leopards.

But the real attraction is the lake itself, a haven of peace. There's a lodge away from the lake, but the lake area is worth camping in and the camps are well equipped. Make your way through the forest to the lakeside and watch the cormorants, herons, pelicans, storks and sandpipers. Enjoy the morning sun with the hippos at Hippo Point.

Drive around to the west side of the lake where you can visit the President's Pavilion on the lakeshore. You'll have a close-

All About Nakuru Ecology
Why do the flamingos favour Nakuru rather than other lakes? The explanation is a perfect ecological cycle. The water comes into the lake through three inlets but has no outlets and so the minerals build up to give the water a high alkaline content.

There are some blue-green algae that thrive on it and the flamingos in turn thrive on the algae. They eat an average of 135 metric tons of algae a day and deposit 45 metric tons of droppings, which in turn decompose and interact with sunlight to enable the algae to double their numbers in a few hours. So the flamingos dine on more algae and it begins again...

There's even a carotene pigment in the algae which adds a pink hue to the flamingo's white feathers. (It's only fair to point out that some years this ecological cycle is upset by excessive rains, which flood the normal lakeshore and make it impossible for the flamingos to wade out to their beloved algae. In which case they fly off to some other lake, so make sure where they are before you plan an excursion.)

Lake Nakuru's best-known attraction is its millions of pink flamingos.

The tranquillity at Lake Nakuru is a lure for both birds and humans, and if you're tired of travelling, you can enjoy it over a cup of tea.

up view of the flamingos in one of their favourite congregating points. (Why else would a president have his pavilion here?) But for a better sense of the sheer immensity of the flamingo phenomenon, go up to the look-out point on Baboon Cliff, also on the western side, for a panoramic view of the whole lake.

The size of **Lake Naivasha** varies according to the rains and it once formed a single lake with Elmenteita and Nakuru. You can go by punt, for hire at the Marina Club, to Crescent Island, a wildlife sanctuary at the eastern end of the lake, and this is by far the most pleasant way to enjoy it. Walk up to the highest point of the island and

you'll have a fine view of the Rift Valley, the Aberdares and the Mau Range.

The lake used to have no fish in it at all, but the Government's wildlife and fisheries department has stocked it with tilapia and black bass, if you want to try your luck from the punt. You'll probably find the shores of Crescent Island too swampy to fish from there. Choose an early week-day morning and you and a few gazelle and tiny dik-dik ante-lopes will be alone with the malachite Kingfisher, pelican, spoonbill and Hottentot teal.

Without the more spectacular beasts of prey as competition, the antelopes are well worth a closer look—they're more delicate and graceful than Walt Disney ever imagined. You may spot a couple of sleepy hippos out in the water. As fascinated as you might be to see them, they, luckily, will be totally bored by you. If you should by the remotest chance **63** come upon a hippo on dry land, be sure not to stand between him and the water. It's the one thing that upsets him. It's his element, not yours. Let him through.

If you are interested in Kenya's prehistoric beginnings, you might like to stop on your way up to Nakuru at the Stone Age sites of Kariandusi and Hyrax Hill. You can see examples of obsidian handaxes and cleavers and some fossilized bones at **Kariandusi,** a palaeolithic campsite perhaps as much as 400,000 years old. **Hyrax Hill** is probably the more interesting of the two sites. A neolithic village of pit dwellings that may be 10,000 years old and a later cemetery in which skeletons were found are visited on the guided tour.

The skeletons were uncovered in a curled-up position, about half of them female. In each case the females were accompanied by utensils, flat stone dishes, platters, mortars and pestles. The males had nothing. Some people have concluded that the burials paid ritual tribute to the fact that the women did all the work. Defenders of the male sex suggest it might merely be that grave robbers carried off the men's belongings. The utensils and other artefacts, including some

beautiful beads, are on view at the small museum.

You can also see a version of the famous *mbao* or *bao* game still played throughout Africa on the hillside site, cut right out of the rock. It consists of two parallel rows of small cavities in which counters, in this case pebbles, are transferred from one to another until captured by one of the two players.

Masai Mara

If your trip to Kenya allows you time for only one game safari, then Masai Mara Game Reserve is almost certainly the place to go. Geographically an extension of Tanzania's world-famous Serengeti National Park, Masai Mara gives you the best chance of seeing all, really all, the major wild animals in a superb rolling landscape of gentle hills, acacia woodland and the sinuous River Mara.

In the heart of Masai land, that is to say land ruled for centuries by pastoralists rather than hunters, the wildlife population has managed to maintain a constant level and now enjoys the protection of an enlightened local authority. Although Masai Mara has the official status of a game reserve and herdsmen are permitted to reside with their cattle, an inner 500 square kilometres, where

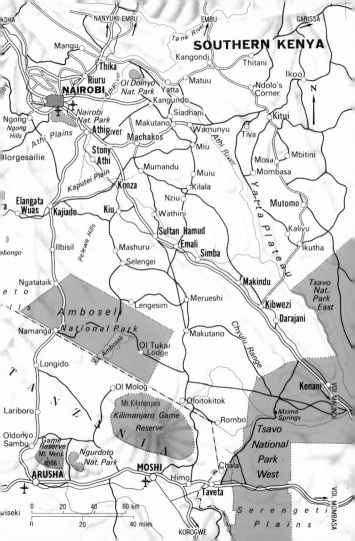

The Masai

While most of Kenyan society has been rushing pell-mell into the 20th century and getting ready for the 21st, the Masai tribe has remained steadfastly conservative, clinging to centuries-old traditions that resist modern institutions. The proud, faintly mocking young warriors *(moran)* with their plaited hair, red cloaks and spears, challenging your curiosity and your camera, recall the fierce reputation the Masai enjoyed in their 19th-century heyday. They fought off Arab slave-traders and rival tribes and intimidated European explorers, before succumbing to the destruction of their cattle by rinderpest and the decimation of their tribe through cholera and smallpox.

The Masai remain committed to cattle-herding as a way of life, living on a diet of milk, tea, maize and blood extracted from their cattle, which they rarely use for meat. During a major drought in the early 1970s they were obliged to leave their traditional grazing lands in search of pasture. They finally found it at Nairobi Airport and the government had a hard time persuading the Masai and their cattle to leave the runways.

The Masai still practise the circumcision and initiation rites that take a male from boyhood to warrior status and then to marriage as an elder. As a warrior he is expected to protect the cattle and the tribe against wild animals—and human beings.

the wildlife is at its densest, is treated as a national park area, excluding all human habitation except for two lodges.

In the north-west, **Mara Serena Lodge** is up on a bluff near the River Mara and looks down over the plain towards the Tanzanian border. From the terrace you can watch the movement of huge herds of migrating buffaloes, zebras, wildebeests and elephants. The lodge is an imaginative modern adaptation of traditional Masai architecture in a "village" of individual huts with external walls of reddish-brown mud (and 20th-century interiors).

Down in the plain at the eastern end of the reserve is **Keekorok,** one of Kenya's oldest game lodges, also laid out with individual accommodation, this time bungalows. Like Mara Serena, it has a swimming pool for the end of a dusty day, but also boasts an artificial water-hole, far enough away for there to be no danger from the elephants and buffaloes it frequently attracts.

If you want to camp among the animals, **Governor's Camp,** by the river in the north-west corner of the reserve, is well-guarded and luxurious enough for the most pampered city-dweller. You'll be plunged into all the sounds and smells of the animal world, and you'll feel very much one of *their* guests.

Driving off the marked tracks across open country is permitted in Masai Mara, but it's advisable to take a Ranger, the Masai being particularly good-humoured companions for the drive. You'll see lots of lions, sometimes in prides up to 20 and 30 strong, and have the best opportunity of sighting a leopard without the aid of a flood-lit baited platform. The open plain is the perfect arena for the cheetah to show his speed. You are likely to find yourself driving through a thicket of acacias out of which a herd of 50 elephants will suddenly materialize. They'll surround your car, but you need not panic—they're more accustomed to you than you are to them. Whatever Mohammed Ali may claim, *they* are the greatest.

Masai are among the handsomest and proudest of Kenya's nomads.

Kericho

Before or after your trip to Masai Mara, particularly if you've spent a long time on the hot, dry and dusty road, you may find yourself for the first time in your life crying out for rain. There's one place that guarantees satisfaction—Kericho with its famous tea plantations about 250 kilometres north-west of Nairobi. There is hardly a day in the year when it doesn't rain. People set their watches by it.

You'll have a morning of brilliant sunshine, not a cloud in the sky at lunchtime, and you'll wonder what local people mean when they say that at 3 p.m. it will rain. Then suddenly the rain comes and you may well be tempted to dance around in the clean, refreshing showers. But first look at your watch: it will almost certainly be 3 p.m.

You can enjoy this spectacle at the Tea Hotel, one of the more elegant vestiges of co-

Tea is by no means a casual local industry. Picked in Kericho's green fields, it's a major export product.

tea-pickers plucking the buds and topmost young leaves and tossing them into wicker baskets on their backs. You can also visit the local tea factories on estates near the town for a fascinating explanation of the cutting, fermenting and drying stages that go into tea processing.

Kenya's tea industry prospered in the 1920s when experts decided Kericho's soil was perfect for producing the best quality tea from Ceylonese and Indian plants. You suddenly realize how the British Empire functioned as a gigantic holding company, enabling the transfer of whole industries from one continent to another. These old imperial origins are neatly underlined by the inscription on a vintage tea-processing machine at one of the factories: "The Britannia Balanced Pucca Tea Sorter (Calcutta, India)".

Kericho is also an excellent centre for fishing expeditions up the Kiptiget River and to the lovely Lower and Upper Saosa Dams, where chances for rainbow trout are good.

lonial times. The unmistakable Englishness of the immaculate green lawns—a welcome change from the arid savannah—is perhaps due to the way the warm sun and sudden rain conjure up nothing so much as the perfect English summer's day. It's altogether fitting that the region produces tea.

The plantations are well worth a visit. There are miles of lush green bushes tightly packed in a shoulder-high carpet dotted with the heads of

Amboseli, Kilimanjaro and Tsavo

Although the wildlife is abundant and easily accessible, the most important reason for recommending **Amboseli National Park** is the simple fact that the elephants, cheetahs and giraffes that you are likely to see there become an unforgettable spectacle against the background of MOUNT KILIMANJARO. Except for the very beginnings of its northern foothills, Kilimanjaro is entirely inside Tanzania, but the awe-inspiring view of it from anywhere in Amboseli makes it an undeniable part of Kenya's landscape, too.

One of the joys of Amboseli is viewing the herds of elephants caked with whitish-grey mud from wallowing in Amboseli's swamps and spraying clouds of dust over their backs. A herd of 40 or more elephants in the mellow evening sun setting over Kilimanjaro is an impressive sight. Naturally, all the wallowing animals in Amboseli turn whitish-grey, except the hippos who wash off their muddy coat.

Elephants take off for Mount Kilimanjaro across the Tanzanian border, leaving us to sit and dream. 71

The most comical of them are the warthogs. These funny little beasts, rarely more than 75 centimetres tall, are dismissed by most people. They remember warthogs from picture books as ugly, even repulsive, because they are usually photographed in close-ups showing those nasty protuberant warts beside each eye and their clumsy little tusks. But when you see them grubbing around as a family, tentatively trying to claim territory at the water-hole while the big brutes are not watching and then, when frightened, scampering away with their tails in the air like tiny flagpoles, warthogs *seem* as endearing as any household pet. They are, however, dangerous and bad-tempered and will not hesitate to charge.

Tsavo National Park, the largest in East Africa, covers about 20,000 square kilometres and is divided into eastern and western sections by the Nairobi–Mombasa highway. After years of drought and forest fires, Tsavo's vegetation has gradually grown back with the aid of newly bored water-

Beauty, they say, is in the eye of the beholder. Behold this warthog.

Kilimanjaro

"As wide as all the world", wrote Hemingway in his famous short story, "great, high and unbelievably white in the sun". The legendary Kilimanjaro is Africa's highest mountain, 5,895 metres. This massive extinct volcano stretches across an 80 by 50 kilometre area and has three marvellous peaks. The highest is the great snow-covered table known as Kibo, but called Uhuru (Freedom) since Tanzania gained independence. The western peak, Shira, is only 4,005 metres and the jagged eastern peak is Mawenzi, 5,150 metres high but much tougher to climb than Kibo. In fact in 1973 a New Zealander went up Kibo on a motorcycle.

Legend has it that the son of King Solomon and the Queen of Sheba, King Menelik of Abyssinia, also made it to the top. In heroic battles he conquered all of East Africa and then, as death approached, he climbed Kibo. He disappeared into the crater with his slaves, who carried all his jewels and treasures, including King Solomon's ring. Find that ring and you'll inherit Solomon's wisdom and Menelik's courage. Failing that, take a good look at one of the great wonders of the world, all the more splendid for standing there alone and unchallenged.

holes. You will see a mixture of dense bush, palm thickets and thorn-tree groves and a less parched savannah than in the bad years of the early 1960s.

The hill country is especially rich in elephants, claiming the largest herds in Kenya. It is not unusual to see a mass of over 100 elephants—still red from their last bath—ambling across a hill in search of water. Solitary giraffes take on a new majesty as they haughtily watch your car curve down the hillside. Once again, you're made to feel an intruder.

The Shaitani lava flow from a volcano extinct only 200 years, at the northern end of Tsavo West, offers an otherworldly landscape. The volcano is said to have buried a Kamba village and as you clamber over the black lava a stretch of your imagination lets you hear beneath the lava, as the legend insists, the Kamba still going about their business with their cattle, goats and dogs.

A cooler, more relaxing experience is yours at MZIMA SPRINGS, where you can see the

Marabou storks, vultures, baboons and ostrich wait around for lunch.

pure, underground water from the Kyulu Hills gush out into limpid pools. The spring provides Mombasa and Malindi with millions of litres of drinking water daily. A crocodile or two can be seen on the banks of the pools—the *far* banks—and the hippos appreciate the purity of the water.

You can watch them at their own level, in a concrete-and-glass underwater observation tank built into one of the pools at the suggestion of a couple of Walt Disney cameramen. You'll also come eye-to-eye with mudsucker fish and bream. Black-faced vervet monkeys scamper through the umbrella thorn-trees and "toothbrush" bushes, the twigs of which can be used for cleaning teeth after a picnic by the Lower Pool.

Tsavo boasts over 500 species of birds, and a lot of them will save you the trouble of searching for them by visiting you on the long terrace at the **Kilaguni Lodge;** the hornbills will particularly welcome a share of your sandwich from the bar. On the road you'll see ostriches running like prim schoolmistresses trying to catch a bus, and the exotic fluffy-headed secretary birds, standing dreamily around unable to take dictation from anyone.

Mombasa and the Coast

The fact that Mombasa is not the capital of Kenya has done nothing to diminish its pride. It has an independent spirit that sets it apart from the rest of the country, and an exoticism derived from its long history and constant contact with the Orient that leaves Nairobi a little jealous. Its climate may be less congenial than the highlands of the interior, but the slower pace adds a languorous fantasy to its streets.

Mombasa has been in existence longer than anyone can remember. Some versions of its history claim that as early as 500 B.C. Phoenician sailors travelling around Africa for the Pharaoh of Egypt put in at a coastal port that would correspond to Mombasa Island. The Greeks noted its trading potential in the first and second centuries A.D., and the Arabs arrived to exploit that potential in the 9th century.

Dhows, carried by the northeast monsoon from the Persian Gulf across the Indian Ocean, made their way along the East African coast looking for an opening in the treacherous coastal reef. The most navigable was at Mombasa, making the city a natural magnet for Arabs, Persians, Turks, Indians, Portuguese and the British, all of whom left their mark on the town.

The island city, linked to the Nairobi road by a causeway, the north mainland by a bridge and the south mainland by a ferry service, is inevitably more Asian than African in its architecture. But the people, the Swahili mixture of fine Arab and lithe African, are a handsome expression of the historic marriage of the two races. You'll find them the blithest of spirits, not easily upset. But this is a demeanour acquired after centuries of fighting off a foreign foe, then absorbing him and fighting off the next one.

When the Portuguese explorer Vasco de Gama arrived at Mombasa in 1498, the people gave him a cold reception and he had to move up the coast to Malindi. It took the Portuguese 100 years of repeated assaults on the island stronghold before they could set up shop for their Indian Ocean trade behind the coral-rock walls of Fort Jesus. That century of Portuguese attack, siege and plunder destroyed medieval Mombasa, and the town we see today is essentially 19th century, except for the remains of Fort Jesus.

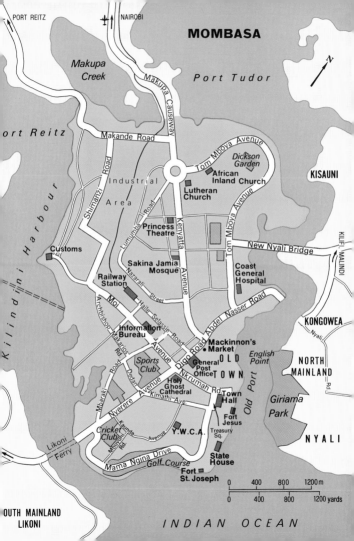

Before you start your tour—and Fort Jesus is the place to start—be warned that the most comfortable way to see the town is to stay outside it and see the sights only in the early mornings and late afternoons. Don't venture out in the mid-day sun.

The one monument you won't miss, coming in or out of town, is the **double arch** across Moi Avenue formed by four huge sheet-metal tusks, which symbolize the source of Mombasa's fortune and misfortunes.

Fort Jesus, strategically placed at the southern entrance to Mombasa Harbour, stands on a coral ridge and has ramparts several metres thick. Inside you can make your way along the parapet walk, step up on the firing positions and imagine what it must have been like to defend this redoubt against marauding infidels—Muslims or Christians or "pagans" according to who held it, since both Portuguese and Arabs made it their stronghold (right up to 1895 when the British took over and turned it into a prison).

With its foundations of solid coral rock, it could not be undermined and any attackers attempting to scale the walls would have been hurled to the dry moat below—now a car park. It was more often taken by guile and bribery than by force.

The ground plan that you see today is much the same as that designed in 1593 by Italian architect Giovanni Battista Cairato for the first Portuguese captain of Mombasa, Mateus Mendes de Vasconcelos, which included a barracks, chapel, water cistern and well, guard rooms, houses for a priest and governor and a storeroom for gunpowder.

During the Arab conquest of the Fort in 1698, the powder magazine was the scene of one of history's recurring acts of mad heroism: a Portuguese officer told the Arabs the storeroom held the garrison's gold treasure, led some Arab soldiers to collect it and blew them and himself to smithereens. The cannons in the courtyard are English 18th- and early 19th-century naval guns brought there in 1837. The Fort also has a museum worth a brief visit. Look at the collection of artefacts from up and down the coast, including Persian, Portuguese and medieval Chinese ceramics, the latter imported from India.

At Mombasa's Old Port, dhows still carry goods to the Persian Gulf.

Behind the Fort, on Treasury Square, is the Government Game Department's **Ivory Room,** where you can see elephant tusks, rhinoceros horns, hippopotamus teeth and other animal trophies confiscated from poachers or taken from dead animals on the reserves. Auctions are held twice a year and you can buy these hot items with legal government permits.

To conserve your energy, limit your walking tour to the **old town.** You'll see the most fascinating part of Mombasa. This area just north of Fort Jesus comprises the mosques, the shops and stalls of silk, spice

This Jain Temple is a fine symbol of the prosperous Indian community.

and perfume merchants, goldsmiths, ivory- and horn-carvers—hustlers all, but with the most amiable of manners. The atmosphere is especially lively at Mackinnon's Market, whose colonial name seems to be resisting the new official title of Municipal Market.

Quickly work your way past the fish market to the **old port** where a sign telling you to "Keep Out" can safely be ignored if you're not part of a big tour group. At the quayside you can watch the loading or unloading of the last of the dhows that still ply between Mombasa and the Gulf. These craft with their large lateen sails, now supplemented by a motor, were once a familiar sight here, coming in with the wind by January and leaving again in June. Now there are just a few dozen.

With a winning smile you may be able to wangle your way aboard and join the haggling for brass chests, Arab silverware, ornate tiles, Persian carpets, furniture, spices and dates. The merchants will be happy to take your money, but their business is usually by barter for ivory, horn, animal skins, sugar, coffee, coconut oil and timber.

The **South Coast,** going down to the Tanzanian border at Tanga, is reached from Mombasa by the Likoni Ferry. This is the only means of transport connecting Mombasa and the beaches of the south. The leisurely ferry takes about ten minutes to travel from the island to LIKONI.

The beauty of the South Coast is in its beaches. The white coral sand is smooth and usually free of seaweed, except in the rainy season, and the beaches are quieter than most of the North Coast's resort areas. The best of the beaches is

the **Diani,** whose major landmark, near the Trade Winds Hotel, is a 500-year-old baobab tree measuring over 20 metres in circumference and protected from felling by presidential decree. Elephants and trees, much more than man-made monuments, are Kenya's protected heritage.

Once you've seen the baobab there is blissfully little to do but watch the sun rise and set, not that sunrises and sunsets here are anything to sneeze at. If you want to give your sun-tan a rest, you can go inland to the little game reserve at **Shimba Hills,** a pleasant wooded plateau rising to 450 metres. Go early in the morning —do everything around here early in the morning or late afternoon—and you should see the splendid sable antelopes with scimitar-shaped horns, rare in Kenya. The males have magnificent coats of reddish-black, while the females are a chestnut-brown colour. There are no lions, so it is safe for the antelopes and you to walk on the higher slopes. But look out for the odd python!

The **North Coast** is where Mombasa's Asian, European and new African élite have their homes, often palatial residences shrouded in hibiscus and bougainvillea and watched over by guard dogs. The area abounds in luxury hotels, for the most part well-run, which will satisfy your every hedonistic need, though some are guilty of exploiting the package-tour trade. The beaches are for the most part clean but some of the hotels are less than efficient about clearing away the seaweed, more prevalent than on the South Coast.

Across the six-lane New Nyali Bridge from Mombasa, the road south leads to ENGLISH POINT, with a monument to the man who explored the Kenya interior on behalf of the British Church Missionary Society, Johann Ludwig Krapf, and the graves of his wife and child.

There are two sets of Arab ruins as you go up to Malindi. The first is at JUMBA LA MTWANA (Home of the Slave-Master), just a couple of miles north of Mombasa. As the town was abandoned in the 15th century, there are only traces of mosques, a characteristic pillared tomb and some houses, one of which was a bakery judging from the large ovens for the baking of millet bread.

The coconuts are ripe and ready to drop. Malindi's smiles are irresistible.

More substantial is the 15th-century town of **Gedi,** close to Malindi. Sunset there is both eery and romantic as you pick your way among the walls of the palace, mosques, houses, pillared tombs and market place. It's likely that the only dramatic event in Gedi's otherwise unremarkable history was its destruction and desertion in the early 1500s, probably during one of Mombasa's wars against Malindi.

Somali tribesmen resettled it briefly at the end of the 16th century but left in a hurry with the news that fierce Galla warriors were on their way south. The palace includes a strong-room where cowrie shells were stored as money. For one gold dinar you had to shell out 40,000 cowries. Another room

in the palace is protected by a *fingo* pot, buried in the floor of the threshold, containing a genie to deal with anyone after the cowries.

Just before you reach Gedi, you'll see the enchanting **Watamu Marine National Park.** Like the nearby Malindi Marine National Park, it is a protected area of white coral sand beaches and clear, deep-blue lagoons, where it is forbidden to fish or collect coral and seashells. Instead you can view these marvels of nature by skin-diving or snorkelling. If you are staying at a hotel in Malindi, you should definitely visit these marine national parks, as the water is as pure as proverbial crystal, whereas the sea at Malindi is for the most part brown with the mud of the Sabaki River.

If you've had a hard year and you just want to sleep for a week or two in the sun, with no demands on your energies, then **Malindi** may be the place **85** for you. You'll have clean beds, wholesome food, swimming-pools and sun-tan lotion. There is some excellent fishing, but it's usually too hot to move around, so you don't have to feel guilty about relaxing until you fly home.

There was a time when Malindi was more lively. With an eye to the main chance, the Sheikh of Malindi decided not to follow Mombasa's hostile example; he received Vasco da Gama hospitably on that 1498 trip and gave him food and water for his voyage to India. It paid off with some golden years of trade with the Portuguese during the 16th century, until Mombasa's resistance was broken and the Portuguese transferred the sheikh there. Malindi then sank back into the torpor that you'll see today.

If you feel up to a short walk, there's a monument to that brief moment of glory out along the cliffs on the promontory at the southern end of the Malindi harbour—the Padrão or Cross of Vasco da Gama, engraved with Portugal's coat of arms and presented to the sheikh by the explorer in gratitude for his warm reception. It has survived the ravages of the Turks, Arabs and British and is one of the few authentic Portuguese relics left on the coast.

For an idea of what Malindi—or Mombasa for that matter—really looked like when the Arabs ruled the coast, you must go up to the island of **Lamu.** "Must" makes it sound like a duty, when in fact it is pure pleasure. Lamu is a delightful backwater of Swahili culture, basking peacefully in splendid isolation at the northern end of the coast. No motor vehicles are allowed other than that of the District Commissioner. People walk about smiling, as if they know something the rest of us don't. And they probably do.

They fish a little and sell some cattle for shipment to Mombasa. Wood-carvers work at their trade and women make their way through the narrow back streets swathed in black *buibuis.* But nobody works too hard. People have a sense of life's priorities on Lamu. They always have time to talk to each other and to strangers. The friendliness is not pushy, not obtrusive, not meant to please a tourist for a tip; it is in the best sense disinterested.

The local inhabitants take pride of place on Lamu; the visitors are always a tiny minority and by no means over-privileged. They have to make their way to the island in small ferry boats, after travelling to nearby MANDA by small aircraft, as the overland route from Mombasa is very rough and often flooded. Once there, visitors are happy to make do with adequate, but never luxurious, lodgings.

The centre of activities, regardless of where you're staying, is the bar at **Petley's Inn.** It's right on the port. This institution is where local people and visitors gather together to talk of cabbages and kings. Nowhere in Kenya do Africans and Europeans mix more easily. Noon and 6 p.m. at Petley's are moments not lightly to be missed. The inn is named after its first owner, Percy Petley, who is said to have thrown unruly women guests down the stairs and to have killed a leopard with his bare hands. Since one version you will hear says he did it by strangling and another with one blow of his fist, probably neither is true.

The most beautiful feature of Lamu's houses is their carved wooden doors and moulded plasterwork. Some of them date back to the 18th century, but even the most modern retain the style, forms and craftsmanship of centuries-old traditions. Some excellent examples are on display in the nicely organized **Lamu Museum.** There are reconstructions of typical Lamu interiors, including a traditional bridal chamber. But the pride of the museum is the two magnificent *sivas* (ceremonial horns), one of carved ivory, two metres long, from Pate Island, and the other of brass, slightly shorter, from Lamu.

There's the fine **Riadha Mosque,** where infidels dressed with due decorum—and without shoes—are admitted. The massive fort built in the early 19th century is now the town prison, which you may look at but not photograph. As the market outside the prison has a lively auction on Saturdays, you could say you were photographing the auction, but it's risky—the prison isn't very appealing inside.

If you want to swim, there's a beach three pleasant kilometres down the road at SHELA, whose Friday Mosque has a distinctive minaret.

Lamu is one island in an archipelago in which Manda and Pate were politically and economically much more important, competing for coastal supremacy and playing foreigners off against each other. They declined while Lamu, quiet and unambitious, survived quite nicely, thank you. There's a moral there somewhere.

What to Do

Sports

Kenya offers the supreme outdoors holiday and opportunities for the sportsman seem endless, despite the current embargo on hunting. **Fishing** is encouraged and there is no closed season. Deep-sea or big-game fishing has taken over from hunting as Kenya's lure for the outdoor man. It's ranked among the best in the world.

At all the breaches in the coral reef up the coast—from the Pemba Channel near the Tanzanian border, to Mombasa, Kilifi, Mtwapa and up to Malindi—you'll find fishing clubs and boat-charter services, many of which have desks at the major hotels. You can rent anything from a little speedboat with an outboard motor to a luxury yacht complete with cabins, showers and fully equipped kitchen. The price, of course, varies greatly. The ho-

tels and fishing clubs will provide you with the indispensable fishing licences. All boats come with an expert crew, rods, reels, bait and all the harness equipment necessary to haul in the big ones.

Do your fishing in the morning and you can expect to grapple with barracudas, kingfish, tunas, marlins, sailfish, dolphins and sharks. Kenya's rivals to *Jaws* include the vicious mako, tiger and hammerhead sharks. Sailfish have been known to come in at over 60 kilos and marlins at over 225. The champion in Kenya waters is a 336-kilo tiger shark, landed in 1973 by a West German after a two-and-a-half-hour struggle.

The best time of year for the biggest fish is November and December, but there isn't really a bad time. Practically all the fishing clubs let you keep everything you catch—if you can eat that much—or you can sell your haul to defray the costs of boat hire.

The peace-loving fishermen on the coast are happy to stand or sit on a rocky promontory and angle their day away half-asleep. You can go surf-casting inside the reef in waters rarely more than thigh deep. There is also good underwater spearfishing for rock-cod.

Inland you can enjoy fine

The intricately carved wooden doors of Lamu Island are coveted by visitors. You can buy replicas.

fishing for rainbow or brown trout in the streams around Mount Kenya, the Aberdares and up at Mount Elgon. Among the best areas near Mount Kenya are the Naro Moru River to the west and the Rupengazi to the east. The trout are delicious at a kilo and may weigh as much as $3\frac{1}{2}$ or $4\frac{1}{2}$. Again, equipment may be hired and you need a licence. The maximum daily bag is six rainbow and four brown trout.

One of the great challenges is fishing for the big Nile perch—weighing up to 90 kilos—in the north at Lake Turkana. You can get equipment at Lake Rudolf Angling Club and Eliye Springs. The perch are also a prime target at Lake Victoria. Lake Naivasha is famous for its black bass and tilapia.

If you prefer to leave the fish where they are, there are other **water sports** to consider. You'll find the coastal waters delightfully warm for swimming, with none of the health risks or crocodiles of the inland rivers and lakes. The sharks stay outside the reef. To explore the coral beds you can hire a wet suit for **skin-diving** or equipment for **snorkelling**. You can also observe sea life from glass-bottomed boats for hire at hotels.

Even if you are a non-swim-mer, you can safely go out to the reef in one of the punts steered by local youths and observe marine life, but note that removing shells is now forbidden. Wear rubber-soled shoes to protect your feet from the razor-sharp coral. There are also several possibilities for **water-skiing** and even a little **surfing** off Malindi.

While you can hire miniature sailboats on the coast, the real **sailing** is done on the tranquil waters of the inland lakes, the best being Naivasha, Nairobi Dam and Lake Victoria (at Kisumu). For the truly adventurous there is **canoeing** on the Tana River.

Riding, an imperial legacy, is most popular in the Highlands. You'll find superb trails in the Ngong Hills, where Danish Baroness Karen Blixen, author of *Out of Africa,* had her farm in the 1920s. It is possible to hire horses, and the best place to enquire is at the Karen *dukas* (shopping centre).

Kenya's thriving bloodstock industry makes for exciting **horse racing.** During the season, which runs from September to July, weekly meets are held most Sunday after-

If tennis strikes you as a bit too strenuous in the coastal heat, you can do nothing at all by the pool.

There are few more peaceful moments on earth than sailing in a dhow around the island of Lamu. You may never want to go back home again.

noons at the Jockey Club of Kenya in Nairobi. Facilities at the track are excellent, and racing enthusiasts claim that the course is one of the most attractive in the world.

Sitting and dreaming at the foot of Mount Kilimanjaro, tantalizingly across the Tan-

zanian border, you may feel the urge to go **mountain climbing.** In which case you have to head for Mount Kenya—at least a thousand others do each year. Thoughtfully providing for the varying abilities of Kenya's tourists, Mount Kenya offers three peaks, each with a dif-

Climbing is organized by the Nairobi-based Mountain Club of Kenya and two Austrian-trained rescue teams are on hand all year round. Climbs begin at the Naro Moru River Lodge, which hires out porters and equipment. Take two days for Lenana and three for Batian or Nelion. There's a longer tour that takes you round all three peaks.

Which brings you to the more conventional sports of **tennis** and **golf,** both well provided for in this former British stronghold, especially in the Highlands. Although there are tennis courts on the coast, have a heart check-up before you play in that heat. The Royal Nairobi, Limuru and Karen golf clubs all accept tourists as guests. The Royal Nairobi's course is of championship calibre and there is a museum commemorating past players in the old-fashioned club-house. The Karen offers parkland greens with a par of 72 and vistas of Nairobi, the Athi Plains and sometimes even Mount Kilimanjaro that may put you off your stroke. Some of them have quaint rules of penalty and compensation if your ball is given a helpful kick or is eaten by a passing animal. In elephant footprints, bunker rules usually apply.

ferent degree of climbing difficulty. The lowest peak, Lenana, rises gently and is within the reach of any reasonably fit person with a head for heights and lungs strong enough to handle the rarefied air at 5,000 metres. If your doctor assures you that you run no risk of pulmonary edema you might even consider the higher peaks. But Batian and Nelion demand expertise rated by professionals as Grades VI and V—Lenana being a mere II.

Photography

Kenya's abundant animals and birds, picturesque peoples, magnificent scenery, colourful flowers and regular sunshine make it a photographer's heaven. Photo safaris are organized in the same way as the old hunting safaris, some of them almost on the scale of Teddy Roosevelt's extravaganzas. You will tour the game reserves and national parks in plush jeeps, bedding down in luxury tented camps complete with iced champagne and the finest cuisine, served by a staff of six or more. Your armed guide will protect you while you wriggle up close to photograph lions and elephants in intimate poses not always possible on the average tour. Certainly by getting away from other tourists, you'll be seeing an Africa closer to the Hemingway dreamland.

But you'll still take some great photographs on the group game-runs led by government rangers in a jeep or minibus. The roof of the minibus will open to give you unimpeded standing shots.

Wild flowers are just as exotic as wild animals—and don't move.

You'll often find the animals so close that your telephoto lens will be a hindrance.

One of the problems of the group runs is that when one vehicle has found a pride of lions basking in the sun after a good meal, other vehicles will rush to the spot and encircle the poor beasts, limiting photographic alternatives. It is a good idea, if the terrain allows it, to pull back from the lions once you've found them and shoot telephoto at a distance in such a way that other groups won't notice your find.

You will occasionally see signs at game reserves forbidding you to take photos of Masai or other tribesmen. This is partly because many of them quite simply object to undignified invasions of their privacy. (Leopards feel that way, too.) But the ban also seeks to avoid the unseemly haggling over payment which many of them not unreasonably ask for posing. You will, however, with proper and discreet preparation find opportunities to photograph the tribesmen in areas where it is not forbidden. You may even find them flagging down your vehicle, to do a dance for you on the road—not exactly *cinéma-vérité* but colourful all the same—for appropriate payment.

Camping

If you can't afford the high-style camping of the luxury photo safaris, there is still a lot of fun to be had camping out in the special sites set aside for those wanting to rough it in the game parks. You can choose from the more than 200 officially recognized campsites throughout Kenya, charging variable (but small) amounts per night. A few are elaborately fitted out with rentable caravans and permanent huts, and have central facilities for cooking, showers, safe drinking water, etc.

There is a scout on hand at most campsites. He is usually armed, but is under strict orders not to shoot an animal except in extreme emergencies. Animals are generally wary of people and should keep their distance unless provoked; but an occasional baboon or vervet monkey might invite himself to dinner if you leave food untended.

Shopping

The big problem in shopping for souvenirs of your stay in Kenya is sorting out the genuine artwork from mass-produced junk. The first rule of thumb is to avoid any shop with a sign that offers "curios". These may well be hand-carved as advertised, but on an assembly line without the careful craftsmanship of the real thing. Authentic, traditional African artwork may be well-nigh impossible to find any more, and your best bets are the wood-carvings at Lamu and replicas of old moulded plasterwork. If these are too pricey, you can also buy the beautifully fashioned brass locks and padlocks made by Lamu locksmiths.

If you do want some of the more modern sculpture, you can find quite good likenesses of elephants, lions or giraffes in wood or soapstone. The best selection will be in Nairobi, rather than out in the countryside. Your best buy on the road is a Masai or Samburu spear or shield. You will also find various versions of the African *mbao* board game (see p. 64) in Nairobi.

In Mombasa shop for antiques—Arab brasswork, trays and "Zanzibar" chests, and carved ivory or horn. You'll find good buys, but nothing will be inexpensive. Animal skins purchased without government

Kenya's best craftwork is as good as any in Africa, but you must be careful to avoid mass production.

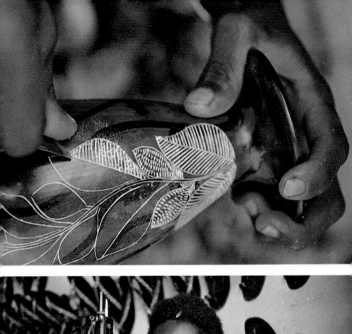

permits—and you won't get one—are strictly illegal.

Crafts cooperatives representing rural artisans have retail shops in the towns. Other important sources of souvenirs are prison industries shops, which are found in most of the major urban centres. You can also recall your stay in Kenya with the safari suits and light cotton or Indian silk *kanga* wraps and dresses that will be tailor-made overnight. However, you may find they lose some of their appropriateness in a European or American context.

Entertainment

The big show is Kenya itself, but if you occasionally have a homesick urge for discotheques or night clubs, Nairobi and Mombasa can satisfy your needs. For the most part you'll be entertained by professional bands, performing European and American pop music with incredible fidelity to the originals, rather than by records.

On the coast the hotels stage disco shows as well as programmes of **native dancing.** But the

Authentic tribal dancing is often hard to find but worth looking for.

latter most often bears the same relationship to the real thing as the "curios" in souvenir shops do to authentic African art. The women wear bras. This is less a sign of prudishness in a European sense than an implicit expression of the incongruity of performing dances with religious or ritually erotic symbolism at a hotel.

A more genuine display of African dancing is available at the Bomas of Kenya near the Nairobi National Park where you can see Samburu war dances, Kamba acrobatics, a Giriama wedding dance and a slightly expurgated version of the Kikuyu circumcision ceremony—still carried on by men though suppressed by women, feminism being a growing movement in Kenya championed by Kenyatta himself and enthusiastically carried forward by the new leadership.

You can gamble at roulette, baccarat and chemin-de-fer at Nairobi's International Casino and watch a Bluebell Girls floorshow to console you for your losses. More decorous entertainment is available in the capital and occasionally elsewhere from various theatre clubs and groups, but Kenya doesn't provide much in the way of European-style night-time entertainment. **99**

Wining and Dining

Wining can be very easily dealt with—drink the beer. Kenya's local brew is excellent, served "cool" or "warm"—that's what they say—according to your preference, as the barman or waiter defers to old colonial tastes. Imported red wines are inevitably over-heated, given the usual room-temperatures, and white wines are refrigerated out of all recognition. Champagne, away from those luxury safaris, is likely to be flat. In hotels and restaurants, all imported wines and spirits are expensive. In shops, wines are expensive, spirits less so. On the coast you might like to try the very potent palm wine. But not at midday.

Dining in Kenya owes much, probably too much, to the colonial past. Most hotels and restaurants offer a faithful and

Without a doubt, the most delicious food in Kenya is the fish at the coast. And nobody ever complained that the portions were too small.

usually unimaginative reproduction of English cuisine, with blandly cooked beef and pork and overdone vegetables.

The great, truly great exception to this is the seafood served on the coast: large succulent spiny lobsters, superb shrimp and prawns—all astoundingly cheap compared with European or American prices—and excellent kingfish and swordfish. If you order them grilled simply, with at most a butter sauce, you will have Kenya's best meals.

Cheeses and desserts, it should be added, are an honourable supplement to the meal, especially with the deli-

cious pineapples and mangoes, though the bananas may seem strange to the European palate. Also, on the game reserves, you will be glad of the English breakfasts served after a dawn game-run.

Nairobi and Mombasa have several fine Indian and Chinese restaurants, and the hotels and lodges do much better with the Indian cuisine than with the English.

African food is a taste perhaps difficult for Europeans and Americans to acquire on a first visit. But the more adventurous might like to try *sukuma wiki na nyama*, sauté of spinach with meat; *kuku wakupaka*, spiced chicken from Lamu; or the ubiquitous *irio*, a Kikuyu mixture of mashed chick peas, maize, pumpkin and potatoes, eaten with meat or fish.

You'll find the service friendly and willing, but sometimes rather over-trained. The waiters have been told to keep your table uncluttered with unused cutlery, plates and glasses and some of these may disappear before you've finished with them. The buffet service favoured by most hotels for at least one of the meals gives you as generous portions as you could wish. In Kenya you eat for energy rather than gourmet delight.

To Help You Order...

Good evening. I'd like
a table for three.

**Habari za jioni. Napenda
kupata meza ya watu watatu.**

I'd like a/an/some...

Nitapenda...

aperitif	**kinywaji kabla ya chakula**	milk	**maziwa**
		potatoes	**mabatata**
beer	**bia [pombe]**	rice	**wali**
bread	**mkate**	rolls	**mkate wa kusukuma**
butter	**siagi**		
cheese	**jibini**	salad	**saladi**
coffee	**kahawa**	salt	**chumvi**
dessert	**chakula mwisho**	seafood	**vyakula vya bahari**
fish	**samaki**		
fruit	**matunda**	soup	**supu**
ice-cream	**aiskrimu**	sugar	**sukari**
lemon	**ndimu**	tea	**chai**
meat	**nyama**	vegetables	**mboga**
mineral water	**maji safi ya kunywa**	(iced) water	**maji (baridi)**
		wine	**divai [mvinyo]**

...and Read the Menu

avokado	avocado	**mbaazi mbichi**	green peas
biringani	aubergine (eggplant)	**mbuzi**	goat
		mchuzi wa nazi	cream of coconut soup
choroko	lentils		
embe	mango	**mtama**	millet
kaa	crab	**ndizi**	bananas
kababu	meat balls	**nyama ya kuponda**	minced meat
karoti	carrots		
kipande cha kondoo	lamb chops	**peschi**	perch
		saladi ya figili	lettuce salad
korosho	cashew nuts		
liiki	leeks	**soseji**	sausages
maji ya matunda	fruit juice	**steki**	steak (in general)
mabalungi/ machungwa	grapefruit/ orange		
		tikitiki maji	melon
nanasi/nyanga	pineapple/ tomato	**tilapia**	a local fresh-water fish

102

How to Get There

From Great Britain

BY AIR: Flights leave daily from London (Heathrow) to Nairobi (some flights are direct to Mombasa), stopping at different places en route according to the day of travel. Passengers from Eire and the provinces must connect at London. There are flights linking Nairobi to Mombasa and other airports in Kenya.

The fares available are first class, economy class, an excursion fare and an APEX (Advance Purchase Excursion) fare. The price of APEX tickets (low compared with other fares) varies according to season—June to September and December to January are considered "high" seasons. You can make stopovers en route with all fares except APEX. Reductions are available for children.

Package Tours: Although there are no charter flights from London to Kenya, package tour operators charter seats on scheduled flights for their clients. A comprehensive range of tours is available, from full board in a top class hotel including safaris, to camping on beaches. Safaris are often organized for groups with special interests like historians, anthropologists and geologists. You may find that package tours which start from other European cities are even cheaper.

Hire cars are available for independent travel in Kenya.

BY SEA: The Canberra World Cruise stops in Mombasa for 47 hours, otherwise there are no cruises or passenger berths on cargo boats available to East Africa from Europe.

BY ROAD: There is a route from Europe to Kenya and you can join overland package holiday groups driving from London to Nairobi.

From North America

BY AIR: Nairobi is serviced by direct flights from New York City on Tuesdays, Thursdays, and Fridays. Connections can be made daily from many American and Canadian cities. Those travelling between New York, Houston or Toronto and Nairobi have the most flights and departure times from which to choose.

Three fares at present available to Kenya are economy, first class, and the 14- to 45-day excursion. The excursion fare is least expensive and can be booked at any time. It permits two stopovers in each direction if the trip is made via Europe. If travel takes place on a weekend, a surcharge must be paid. Children 2 to 11 years of age fly for 50% of the adult excursion rate.

Charter Flights and Package Tours: A variety of Group Inclusive Tours (GIT), usually of three weeks' duration, combines visits to cities like Capetown, Cairo and Casablanca with wildlife tours of Kenya. Several programmes include Brazil as the first stopover point. From there, travel is due east to South Africa and then north to Victoria Falls, Kenya, and the Sudan. Included in the cost of the tour are roundtrip air transport transfers, accommodation at de luxe hotels and lodges, all or most meals, tips, and the services of a guide. A 15-day OTC (One-Stop Inclusive Tour Charter) has been designed for the traveller who wants to visit only Kenya and to spend nine days on safari.

If you wish to enter Kenya after a visit to the Republic of South Africa, you may have difficulty depending on your nationality. Check with your own embassy in Kenya before you decide on your route.

When to Go

Since Kenya is on the Equator, climate remains pretty stable throughout the year. Temperatures in Nairobi, the Highlands and other mountainous areas are modified by the altitude; days are generally sunny and hot but nights can be cool. Note, also, that temperature can vary significantly between day and night. The following charts give you an idea of the average monthly temperatures and rainfall in two different areas of Kenya. Water temperature remains fairly constant all year—from 23 °C (73 °F) to 26 °C (79 °F).

Nairobi	J	F	M	A	M	J	J	A	S	O	N	D
°C max.	26	27	27	26	24	23	23	23	26	26	25	25
min.	13	13	14	15	15	13	12	12	13	14	14	14
°F max.	79	81	81	79	75	73	73	73	79	79	77	77
min.	55	55	57	59	59	55	54	54	55	57	57	57
Rainfall (in inches)	2	3	5	8	6	2	1	1	1	2	4	3

Mombasa	J	F	M	A	M	J	J	A	S	O	N	D
°C max.	32	32	32	31	29	29	28	28	29	30	31	31
min.	23	24	24	24	22	22	21	21	21	22	23	23
°F max.	90	90	90	88	84	84	82	82	84	86	88	88
min.	73	75	75	75	72	72	70	70	70	72	73	73
Rainfall (in inches)	1	1	3	8	13	5	4	3	3	3	4	2

Planning Your Budget

To give you an idea of what to expect, here are some average prices in Kenya Shillings. They should be considered only as guidelines, however; inflation is as rampant in Kenya as elsewhere.

Air charters. 5-passenger plane (single) Shs. 2,344/50 per hour, 8-passenger plane (twin) Shs. 4,490/–.

Airports. Airport buses to Mombasa and Nairobi city centres Shs. 30/–, taxis to most central Nairobi hotels Shs. 162/–, porters Shs. 5/– to 10/–, departure tax U.S.$10 (to be paid in freely convertible currency).

Baby-sitters. Shs. 20/– per hour plus transport.

Camping. In Masai Mara booking fee of Shs. 1,000 plus Shs. 50 per person per night, in other National Parks and Reserves Shs. 30/– per person per night.

Car hire (Nairobi). Smallest saloon Shs. 150/– per day, Shs. 2/50 per km., Shs. 3,600/– per week with unlimited mileage. Microbuses (with chauffeur) Shs. 400/– per day, Shs. 5/– per km. Insurance extra.

Cigarettes (per packet of 20). Local brands Shs. 3/– to 10/–, locally manufactured foreign brands Shs. 18/–, imported brands Shs. 25/–.

Hairdressers. *Man's* barber cut Shs. 30/– to 40/–. *Woman's* haircut Shs. 80/– to 150/–, shampoo and set Shs. 100/– to 120/–, blow-dry Shs. 75/–, permanent wave Shs. 380/– to 500/–.

Hotels. Luxury, double room Shs. 1,170/–, single Shs. 920/–. First class, double room Shs. 390/–, single Shs. 250/–. Second class, double room Shs. 250/–, single Shs. 175/–. Third class, double room Shs. 95/–, single Shs. 70/–.

Meals and drinks (medium-priced restaurant). Breakfast Shs. 40/– to 50/–, lunch (set menu) Shs. 75/– to 85/–, dinner (set menu) Shs. 120/–, coffee Shs. 8/50, beer (½ litre) Shs. 9/85, soft drinks Shs. 3/50, brandy Shs. 36/–, other spirits Shs. 25/–, wine Shs. 28 per glass, fresh fruit juice Shs. 15/– per glass.

Sports. Game fishing Shs. 1,800– per day. Offshore fishing and goggling/snorkelling Shs. 100/– per hour. Water-skiing Shs. 7/– per minute. Windsurfing Shs. 140/– per hour. Scuba diving, beginner's course Shs. 600/–, experienced divers Shs. 150/– per hour. 7-day saddle safari Shs. 3,000/–, 10-day camel safari Shs. 4,500/–.

Trains. Private first-class compartment for two, per person (single occupancy + 50%), Nairobi to Mombasa Shs. 340/–, to Kisumu Shs. 354/–. Return ticket double.

BLUEPRINT for a Perfect Trip

An A-Z Summary of Practical Information and Facts

A star (*) following an entry indicates that relevant prices are to be found on page 106.

Contents

A   **AIR CHARTERS***. Chartering an aircraft has not been till now a millionaire's prerogative in Kenya—mercifully, since distances are vast and roads forbidding. A few hours' flight to Lake Turkana, instead of several days' ride on an endurance-testing, backbreaking bus, may mean saving more than time alone. This pleasant situation is, however, fast degenerating, owing to the oil crisis in the Middle East.

Kenya Airways have regular flights to Mombasa and Malindi. In addition there are several charter airlines, which have turned Nairobi's Wilson Airport into Africa's busiest. Cessnas, Pipers and Beechcrafts buzz in and out of the airport at two-minute intervals during peak hours and serve the more than 200 airstrips that dot the Kenyan countryside. Most hotels and lodges outside the main urban centres have landing strips nearby.

Sunbird (see below) operate regular flights from Nairobi's Wilson Airport to Lamu, Masai Mara and Kisumu.

Other large charter airlines based at the Wilson Airport are Boskovic Air Charters and Air Kenya.

Addresses:

Boskovic Air Charters: P.O. Box 45646, Nairobi; tel. 501210/9.

Safari Air Services Ltd.: P.O. Box 41951, Nairobi; tel. 501211.

Air Kenya: P.O. Box 30357, Nairobi; tel. 501601/2/3/4.

Sunbird Charters: P.O. Box 44580, Nairobi; tel. 501319/501467.
            P.O. Box 82, Nanyuki; tel. 2053.
            P.O. Box 87669, Mombasa; tel. 21679.

AIRPORTS*. Kenya is served by two of the largest, most modern and efficient international airports in Africa. The Jomo Kenyatta International Airport is half-an-hour's drive from Nairobi's city centre, where most of the better hotels are located. Mombasa's Moi International Airport on the Kenya coast is closer to the town centre, but most of the tourist hotels are at various distances from the town.

At both airports, electronic conveyor belts ferry baggage close to customs officials, and there are teams of porters ready to carry heavy bags to the customs zone without charge. Another team of porters will carry luggage beyond customs to bus stops and taxi stands for modest tips.

There are banks, car hire offices, hotel reservation desks, duty-free shops, gift shops, newsagents stocking international and local magazines and newspapers, post offices, long distance telephone services, **108** pharmacies (drugstores) and bars and restaurants at both airports.

Most tourist hotels have their own minibuses at the airports to transport guests, while airlines provide transport to terminals in the city centres. Kenya Airways buses leave on the hour to a central terminal, stopping at main hotels on the way and every hotel within Nairobi. A public bus serves both the Jomo Kenyatta and Moi airports. Numerous taxis are on hand.

Kenya Airways buses leave the city-centre terminals (at Sadler House, Koinange Street, Nairobi; and Jubilee Building, Moi Avenue, Mombasa) on the hour.

There is an airport tax for departing passengers.

BABY-SITTERS★ *(msaidizi wa kutazama mtoto)*. Most hotels will arrange baby-sitting services for their guests. Rates vary widely depending on the location of the hotel or lodge, and on the number of children, but are never excessive.

CAMPING★. Camping is a way of life in the warm Kenyan sun, and some people would say it is the only way to experience the real Kenya. Wherever you want to camp, you are certain to be surrounded by magnificent scenery, and in some places, by a wide range of wildlife. There is even a campsite with good facilities in the Nairobi City Park. You can book sites on the spot or at the town hall.

Camping has become a thriving "extra" for Kenya's tour operators, and the better-off visitor can experience the thrill of Kenya's vast skies and the *bundu*—the endless bush—at a comfortably fitted campsite that serves champagne for breakfast! But for the adventurous and the enterprising visitor (and resident alike), camping in Kenya's wild bushlands can be an inexpensive and delightful do-it-yourself holiday, and an unforgettable experience.

Find a site well before sunset, for in tropical Africa it can be pitch dark half-an-hour after the sun starts to go down. Choose level ground with short grass and plenty of shade, but beware of the type of tree you camp under: thorn trees are good for shade and have no climbing leopards and snakes, but underneath them there is usually a thick carpet of thorns; some trees exude sap, and trees with lots of bird nests mean there will be unwelcome bird droppings.

In hot, low-altitude areas, temperatures inside a tent can be unbearably high, so make sure the rear windows face the prevailing wind.

Do not set camp on, or too near, a sandy expanse of a dry riverbed—a tropical rainstorm miles away can send unbridled water gushing down towards you.

109

C

Avoid camping right across or too near a game trail. Not only might your tent attract some unnecessary curiosity, but you could find an animal stumbling into your guy ropes.

There is always the danger of a fire going wild. Learn to build "safe" fires, with stones around the campfire, and keep the flames under control at all times.

Camping equipment: if you intend spending the whole holiday under canvas, bring as much equipment as your light-weight allowance will permit, although you can actually, in case of need, buy or rent supplies in Nairobi at very attractive prices.

The main items include: tent (with a sewn-in groundsheet and mosquito-netted windows); camp beds (airbeds are vulnerable to thorns), sleeping bags; folding chairs and table; local pots and pans (Kenyan lightweight ones are excellent for direct fire use); plastic airtight containers for bread, sugar, salt, etc.; axe and machete; *karai* —a wide metal bowl useful for heating water, for washing, or covering the fire when it rains; a two-burner gas stove with spare gas; torch (flashlight); plates, mugs, spoons, knives, kitchen knives; folding spade; wooden board for cutting bread and vegetables; gas lamps; insulated boxes; personal equipment; binoculars; plenty of drinking water; food (which you need to plan with care depending on which part of the country you are heading towards); appropriate safari clothes.

CAR HIRE*. Nairobi boasts more than 200 car hire firms. This says more about Kenya's spirit of free enterprise than about the state of the car hire business in the country. At the airports and hotels you'll see the familiar names. But look through the phone book first and see what other companies there are before you make arrangements. Prices are generally higher than in Europe and North America. A tour agent or hotel concierge can help you select the firm that best suits your needs and pocket.

Before you hire a car, be aware of the many deterrents to self-drive (see DRIVING).

CIGARETTES, CIGARS, TOBACCO* *(sigara, sigaa, tumbaku).* Imported European and American cigarettes are available in the large towns and cities, but are generally dearer than at home. Cheaper local brands are made to surprisingly high quality. Bring your own cigars.

A packet of…/A box of matches, please.

Pakiti ya …/Kibiriti, tafadhali.

filter-tipped/without filter   **zenye filta/isioyo na filta**

CLIMATE and CLOTHING. See also page 105. Temperatures in Nairobi and throughout the highlands are never excessive, thanks to high altitudes, but bear in mind, nevertheless, that Nairobi is only 60 miles south of the Equator and that the sun can be strong. Those not acclimatized should wear hats. Evenings are cool and can be chilly. Warm clothing is therefore necessary after sunset, especially on safari.

On the coast, beachwear is sufficient for day-time in hotels, with a loose cotton dress or shirt worn to meals or when walking or shopping. Nylons and other synthetic materials prove very hot for the coast; cotton is much more suitable. Incidentally, nudity on the beaches or in any public place is against the law in Kenya.

COMMUNICATIONS. Post offices are indicated by the letters PTT (Post, Telephone, Telegraph). Mail boxes are painted red. You can also buy stamps at stationers, souvenir shops and small grocers' shops.

Post office hours: From 8 a.m. to noon and from 2 to 4.30 p.m., Monday to Friday, from 8 a.m. to noon only on Saturdays.

Poste Restante (General Delivery): Letters can reach you, but the system in Nairobi is a little haphazard. At the post office on Kenyatta Avenue you ask for the letters beginning with your initial and look through the bunch for your mail. Since the clerk is not very strict about checking your identity, you may find letters "going astray". It's best to have mail sent to a listed address, but allow plenty of time. An airmail letter from Europe can take between three and ten days, from the U.S.A. sometimes as long as two to three weeks.

Telegrams: These can be sent by telephone through the operator. Ask at the information office or hotel reception desk for the nearest telex facilities. When possible, it is recommended to send messages by telex.

Telephone: From Kenya you can dial directly only to Uganda and Tanzania. Long distance calls outside East Africa have to be placed through the operator.

City telephone kiosks are painted red. If you cannot locate one, or if you find one out of order, approach the nearest hotel, restaurant or shop; they will allow you to use their telephone at double the normal rate. Long distance calls are cheaper between 6 p.m. and 6 a.m.

CONVERTER CHARTS. For fluid and distance measures, see page 113. Kenya uses the metric system.

C Temperature

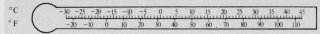

Length

Weight

grams / ounces scale

CRIME and THEFTS. There are some areas in Nairobi and Mombasa where it is inadvisable to wander after dark. Avoid going into poorly lit areas or buildings in the towns, or strolling alone on empty highways, lanes or on the beaches at night.

Remember that Kenya is still a country of great contrasts in wealth, with most of the African population living on very modest means. Do not carry large sums of cash or traveller's cheques on you. Deposit what you do not require immediately with the manager of your hotel for safe-keeping. Lock all articles in the boot of your car, and lock the car too. Similarly, do not leave valuable personal belongings unattended on beaches and in public places.

If you feel in the slightest worried, you should discuss the current local situation with your hotel manager or your tour leader.

D DRIVING IN KENYA.

DRIVING IN KENYA. To drive a hired car in Kenya all you need is a valid international driving licence. But bear in mind that this is the home of the famous Safari Rally, designed to test to the limit the endurance and toughness of both the driver and the car. Roads are being improved all the time and at a faster rate than in many other African countries, but if you are on holiday, you may want to leave much of the driving, especially on the off-beat sandy and muddy roads, to experienced and well-trained tour drivers.

Although it's rather unlikely that you'll ship your car to Kenya, if you do, you would be wise to check beforehand how long you are allowed to use it without having to pay import duty. Have it cleared by customs as soon as it arrives, or you'll have heavy storage charges to pay. To take your car into Kenya you will need:

- an international driving licence
- car registration papers
- an international insurance certificate
- a nationality plate or sticker

Driving conditions: As an inheritance of the British past, Kenyan motorists drive on the left and overtake (pass) on the right. Most vehicles have the steering wheel on the right. Roads are generally narrow, so make sure you have full view of the stretch ahead before you attempt to overtake.

Driving in the national parks: Speeds are strictly limited to 30 or even 20 m.p.h. (50 or 30 k.p.h.), so as not to frighten the wild animals. For the same reason all loud noises and brusque movements should be avoided, both when driving and while taking photographs. Don't try to nudge animals out of the way; just enjoy the occasion and wait for them to move on.

Fluid measures

imp. gals.	0	5	10
litres	0	5	10	20	30	40	50
U.S. gals.	0	5	10

Distances: Here are some approximate road distances in kilometres between major centres:

Nairobi–Eldoret	310	Mombasa–Eldoret	800
Nairobi–Kisumu	350	Mombasa–Kisumu	845
Nairobi–Malindi	615	Mombasa–Malindi	120
Nairobi–Marsabit	560	Mombasa–Marsabit	1,110
Nairobi–Mombasa	490	Mombasa–Moyale	1,380
Nairobi–Nanyuki	200	Mombasa–Nakuru	650
Nairobi–Nyeri	160	Mombasa–Namanga	605

To convert kilometres to miles:

| km | 0 | 1 | 2 | 3 | 4 | 5 | 6 | 8 | 10 | 12 | 14 | 16 |
| miles | 0 | ½ | 1 | 1½ | 2 | 3 | 4 | 5 | 6 | 7 | 8 | 9 | 10 |

D **Traffic violations:** For minor traffic offenses the police usually impose fines on the spot against your signature on a sheet admitting the charge. Send your cheque by registered post to the address of the traffic court given on your charge sheet. Following this procedure can save you a great deal of time, for local traffic courts are quite busy.

Breakdowns: Before setting out for long-distance driving, get in touch with the Automobile Association of Kenya, with headquarters in Nairobi. The A.A. will advise on the road conditions ahead, and on how you can obtain help in case of emergency.

Telephones:		
	Nairobi:	720382/3
	Mombasa:	26778
	Eldoret:	2700
	Kisumu:	41361
	Nakuru:	2314

Are we on the road to…?	**Tuko katika njia sawasawa ya kwenda…?**
Fill the tank, please.	**Tafadhali jaza tangi.**
normal/super	**standardi/premium**
I've had a breakdown.	**Imeniharibikia nilipokuwa.**
There's been an accident.	**Kumetokea ajali.**

E **ELECTRIC CURRENT.** Major towns and cities are supplied with 240 volts, 50 cycles A.C. Some lodges have independent power generators which vary in voltage.

Tourist hotels and lodges generally provide an adaptor for 220 and 110 volts. The plug in use throughout Kenya is of the three-pin 13-ampere type.

EMBASSIES, CONSULATES, HIGH COMMISSIONS. Kenya maintains diplomatic relations with more than 80 countries.

Australia:	High Commission: Development House, Government Road, P.O. Box 30360, Nairobi. 334666/334620.
Canada:	High Commission: Comcraft House, Haile Selassie Avenue, P.O. Box 30481, Nairobi. Tel. 334033.
Eire:	Embassy: Monrovia Street, P.O. Box 30659, Nairobi. Tel. 26771.

United Kingdom:	High Commission: Bruce House, Standard Street, P.O. Box 30465, Nairobi. Tel. 335944/60.
U.S.A.:	Embassy: Moi Avenue, P.O. Box 30137, Nairobi. Tel. 334141.

Denmark:	Embassy: H.F.C.K. Building, Koinange Street, P.O. Box 40412, Nairobi. Tel. 331088.
	Consulate: E.A. Storage Co., Ltd., Shimanzi, P.O. Box 95119, Mombasa, Tel. 314333/4.
Finland:	Embassy: Diamond Trust House, Moi Avenue, P.O. Box 30379, Nairobi. Tel. 334777/8.
Netherlands:	Embassy: Uchumi House, Nkrumah Road, P.O. Box 41537, Nairobi. Tel. 332420.
	Consulate: Nedlloyd EA Ltd., Moi Avenue, P.O. Box 80149, Mombasa, Tel. 311043.
Norway:	Embassy: H.F.C.K. Building, Koinange Street, P.O. Box 46363, Nairobi. Tel. 337121.
	Consulate: Ralli House, Nyere Avenue, P.O. Box 86954, Mombasa. Tel. 311404.
Sweden:	Embassy: International House, Mama Ngina Street, P.O. Box 30600, Nairobi. Tel. 29042/3/4/5.
	Consulate: Southern House, Moi Avenue, P.O. Box 86108, Mombasa. Tel. 20501.

EMERGENCY and SERVICES TELEPHONE NUMBERS

Police, Fire, Ambulance anywhere in Kenya	999
Police Headquarters, Nairobi area	22251
St. John's Ambulance, Nairobi	22396/24066
Time	993
Long-Distance Calls	0196
Dialling Assistance	900
Nairobi Airport Information	822111

ENTRY FORMALITIES and CUSTOMS CONTROLS. Citizens of Great Britain (except passport holders of Indian and Pakistani origin), Eire, Canada and New Zealand are entitled to a three-month visitor's pass, and no visas are required. The same applies to citizens of a **115**

E limited number of other countries. All other nationalities should obtain visas from one of the embassies, consulates or consular representatives in their countries. Most travellers en route from South Africa are refused entry to Kenya, but permitted to transit providing they do not leave the airport. A deposit (refundable on departure) of the equivalent of £250 sterling per person may be required upon arrival, but visitors holding a ticket for the return or onward journey are normally exempt from this. Visitors are also required to carry a minimum sum of £200 sterling or the equivalent in a convertible foreign currency.

The following chart shows what main duty-free items you may take into Kenya and, when returning home, into your own country.

Into:	Cigarettes	Cigars	Tobacco	Spirits	Wine
Kenya	200	or 50	or 250 g.	1 l.	or 1 l.
Australia	200	or 250 g.	or 250 g.	1 l.	or 1 l.
Canada	200	and 50	and 900 g.	1.1 l.	or 1.1 l.
Eire	200	or 50	or 250 g.	1 l.	and 2 l.
N. Zealand	200	or 50	or ½ lb.	1 qt.	and 1 qt.
U.K.	200	or 50	or 250 g.	1 l.	and 2 l.
U.S.A.	200	and 100	and *	1 l.	or 1 l.

* a reasonable quantity

Currency restrictions: Import and export of Kenya Shillings is not permitted. You can bring any amount of foreign currency into Kenya, but it must be declared upon arrival. Great care must be taken of the declaration form which will be required on departure. Leaving the country, you can take with you up to the equivalent of 4,000 Kenya Shillings, provided the amount is entered in your passport.

G **GUIDES and INTERPRETERS.** Trained tour guides and interpreters have been graduating from the Kenya Utalii (Tourism) College (the only such centre in Black Africa) since 1974; but there is still a serious shortage of guides. All available are employed by the tour companies and hotels and their charges are included in hotel or tour bills.

HITCH-HIKING. This is not yet a very practical way of travelling in Kenya, except on the Nairobi–Mombasa Highway. Outside towns, vehicles are still extremely rare. But if you have the patience to wait, your patience may well be rewarded by some kindly motorist.

Can you give me a lift to…?	**Unaweza kunichukua garini kwenda…?**
Where to?	**Wapi?**

HOTELS and ACCOMMODATION*. Kenya's hotels and lodges are classified in four categories. The luxury hotels offer extremely high standards of service and are comparable to the best hotels anywhere in the world with rates on an international scale. First-class hotels offer comfortable accommodation, efficient services, a variety of international dishes or specialized dishes of various nations, and all rooms have private bath and toilet, telephone, radio and television. Second class hotels and lodges offer reasonable comfort and a range of European-type food, and they generally have showers in rooms. Third-class hotels and lodges are not recommended for tourists; services are limited.

Kenya also has a few motels that offer good accommodation, food and reasonable services for the motorist. In many urban centres, there are guest or boarding houses for those who want to stay for extended periods. Some of these boarding houses are extensions of large hotels.

On the coast a large number of comfortably furnished bungalows can be found, usually near beaches, for families and groups who desire a homely atmosphere and who want to do their own cooking.

Most hotels offer a reduction of 50% for children under 12. At the height of the tourist season, hotel accommodation in Kenya can be scarce, so an early reservation—and confirmation—is always advisable. But if stuck without a room, ask for the tourist information office, which you will find in most major towns throughout the country.

Where is the tourist information office?	**Wapi ofisi ya habari kwa watalii?**

LANGUAGE. Swahili, the lingua franca of East Africa, was originally written in Arabic characters. When British missionaries introduced the Latin alphabet, they adopted as phonetic a transliteration as possible, so that Swahili is rather easy to pronounce. Kenyans also speak more than forty tribal languages. Most educated people, however, speak English remarkably well, and so English, whatever accent you have, will be understood, except well off the beaten track, where you'll need

L Swahili. The Berlitz phrase book SWAHILI FOR TRAVELLERS will help you get by in just about any situation you're likely to meet.

Hello	**Jambo**
Good morning	**Habari za asubuhi**
Good afternoon	**Habari za alasiri**
Good evening	**Habari za jioni**
Good night	**Lala salama**
Please/Thank you	**Tafadhali/Asante**
You're welcome	**Karibu**
Goodbye/See you soon	**Kwa heri/Tutaonana**

LAUNDRY and DRY-CLEANING *(dobi mfua nguo; dobi wa nguo za sufu)*. Hotel laundry is generally done well and, if you insist, overnight. If you are in central Nairobi, you may want to try one of the many fast-service dry-cleaners. Ask at the reception desk for the one nearest your hotel.

I want these clothes...	**Nataka nguo hizi...**
cleaned	**zisafishwe**
ironed	**zipigwe pasi**
pressed	**zipigwe pasi**
washed	**zioshwe**
I need them...	**Nazitaka...**
today/tonight/tomorrow	**leo/usiku/kesho**

M **MAPS.** Most of the hotel stationery shops are well stocked with brightly illustrated maps of city centres, game parks, campsites, roads, etc. Maps are distributed by tourist information offices in the major towns. In Nairobi and Mombasa, precise but complicated maps can be obtained from the Land's Offices.

MEDICAL CARE

Vaccinations: Yellow fever and cholera inoculations are advisable, but obligatory only if you enter from an infected area.

You can safely swim in the sea, but avoid swimming, bathing in or drinking from lakes (especially Lake Victoria), rivers or open natural reservoirs because of the risk of bilharzia, parasites, typhoid or dysentery bacilli (a vaccination against typhoid and paratyphoid fevers is recommended). All swimming pools are safe and usually well cared for.

Malaria is still a problem all over the country. Nairobi is officially malaria-free, but don't run unnecessary risks; take one of the many reliable prophylactics for two weeks before you arrive in Kenya, all the time you are in the country, and for four to six weeks after you return home. Consult your doctor.

Insurance: If your medical insurance cannot be extended to foreign countries, you may want to take out special travel insurance to cover yourself in case of accident, illness or hospitalization during your trip.

Doctors: There are highly qualified doctors, surgeons and dentists in both Nairobi and Mombasa.

Doctors' surgeries are open from 8 a.m. to 5 p.m., some till 6 p.m. or later. Lodges in remote game reserves have resident medical staff. The lodges have radio or telephone contact with the Flying Doctor Service in Nairobi. If travelling under your own steam, camping, etc., you should think of joining the Flying Doctor Service as a temporary member for a small fee. The "Flying Doctors" have a legendary reputation for daring rescue missions all along the east coast of Africa.

Pharmacies: Pharmacists in the major urban centres take turns to stay open late—till about 9 p.m.; rosters are published daily in the newspapers. Pharmacies at the major hospitals remain open 24 hours a day.

Hospitals: The major hospitals in the **Nairobi** area are all well-equipped:

The Kenyatta National Hospital is the nerve centre of Kenya's hospital system and a university teaching hospital. Large and modern. Tel. 334800.

Nairobi Hospital, private and expensively fitted out, offers the most modern equipment and comfort, as well as an impressive number of highly qualified consultants. Tel. 722160.

Gertrude's Garden specializes in children's illnesses. Tel. 65305.

The Aga Khan Hospital boasts a large team of resident doctors. Tel. 742531.

Mater Misericordiae Hospital specializes in maternity and related cases. The hospital is run by an order of Catholic sisters and is noted for excellence in nursing care. Tel 556666.

The major hospitals in the **Mombasa** area are fully equipped:

The Coast General Hopital is the largest. Tel. 314201.

The Katherine Bibby Hospital is comfortable and expensively fitted out. Tel. 312191.

M **Health precautions:** Visitors heading for the coast are advised to take all things in moderation at the start. There is a clinical condition known as "heat exhaustion" which is generally brought about by an excess of eating or drinking, sun-bathing or exercising, not just by temperature. Although sunstroke is rare on the coast, sunburn is very common. Bring your favourite suntan cream with you.

MEETING PEOPLE. By and large, Kenyans are friendly and easy-going, perhaps more so in Mombasa than elsewhere. In Nairobi, people are courteous but a little more businesslike in their manner. In the countryside there is a certain shyness, but this derives more from the unfamiliarity of English or other European languages—or even Swahili as opposed to local dialects—than from any unwillingness to communicate. In Nairobi, the most likely place for you to meet with African or European residents is at the New Stanley's "Thorn Tree" (see p. 32). In Mombasa the discos and other nightclubs are frequented by Europeans and Africans alike. Probably the best place in all of Kenya for meeting people is the island of Lamu, especially down by the harbour at Petley's Inn.

MONEY MATTERS

Currency: Kenya's unit of currency is the Shilling (abbreviated Sh(s), written 1/–, 2/50, etc.), divided into 100 cents (c). There are copper coins of 5 and 10c and silver coins of 50c and Sh 1/–. Banknotes come in denominations of Shs 5/–, 10/–, 20/–, 50/– and 100/–. It is an offence to deface or damage Kenya currency in any way. For currency restrictions, see ENTRY FORMALITIES AND CUSTOMS CONTROLS.

Exchange control regulations: Visitors are particularly warned against those "unofficial" money changers who will offer incredible deals in the street—you will be breaking the law and will usually end up with a handful of paper or forged notes. Foreign currency, including traveller's cheques, may be exchanged for cash only at a commercial bank or an authorized hotel. It may also be used for purchases of goods from persons licensed to accept foreign currency.

Banking hours: Banks in Nairobi and the major towns west of Nairobi open from 9 a.m. to 2 p.m., Monday to Friday, from 9 a.m. to 11 a.m. on the first and last Saturday of the month. Banks in Mombasa and along the hot coastal belt open and close half an hour earlier. Some of the banks at the international airports open round the clock every day, while others begin at 6 a.m. and go on till midnight every day.

Foreign exchange departments of major banks in Nairobi stay open till 4.30 p.m. from Monday to Friday. You can also change money in most of the major hotels and resorts throughout the country, but at a slightly disadvantageous rate.

Credit Cards and Traveller's Cheques: Only a small number of international credit cards are accepted in Kenya. Traveller's cheques are readily recognized and accepted at most international hotels and tourist agencies.

Prices: Visitors are often surprised by the high prices, particularly of imported items, of goods in the shops, but there are very heavy import duties and sales tax. If you consider that you are being exploited, consult your tour leader or travel agent.

NEWSPAPERS and MAGAZINES. Kenya has three well established English-language daily papers, the *Nairobi Times,* the *Nation* and the *Standard,* and their Sunday counterparts. There is also a weekly English-language magazine and a wide range of monthlies. Many international newspapers and magazines are sold on newspaper stands and in stationer's shops in the large hotels several days later—unless you come across private entrepreneurs who pick up second-hand copies left by travellers at airports and re-sell them for the full cover price.

PHOTOGRAPHY. Well-known brands of film are on sale, but prices are higher than in Europe and the United States. You will need high-speed film for animal shots. Zooms are useful and telephoto lenses essential for good wildlife photography in Kenya. A 135-mm. lens is sufficient for animals, perhaps a 200-mm. for birds. Some Nairobi and Mombasa photo shops have good selections of still or cine cameras for sale or hire.

Your camera will require more than usual protection. While in the bush on dusty roads, keep camera and lenses in polythene bags, preferably shopping bags, where they can be reached easily. The dust goes everywhere, even into tightly closed car boots. Do not leave your camera in the sun or locked in your car in the heat; the colours will be washed out of the film. Keep it away from sand and salt water. And when you go through security checks don't allow your camera and film to be submitted to detection devices; Kenyan authorities will readily examine these separately.

It is forbidden to photograph the national flag, the president, state lodges, soldiers, prison officers, prisoners, prison establishments and (for the time being) the late President Kenyatta's mausoleum. Failure

P to observe this regulation will invariably cost you your film or even camera, and may lead to a court fine.

Some of Kenya's more colourful tribespeople have become wise to tourist ways and may demand a small fee to pose for a photograph.

Can I take a picture?   **Naweza kupiga picha?**

POLICE. All policemen and policewomen are friendly and helpful to tourists and are the most reliable source of any kind of information you require. There are various branches of the Kenya Police, but the two types you are likely to meet are the traffic and the criminal police. If they cannot help you, they will tell you where to obtain the information you need. They are also the most efficient source of help in case of emergency of any kind.

To reach a policeman in an emergency, dial 999.

PUBLIC HOLIDAYS

January 1	New Year's Day
May 1	Labour Day
June 1	Madaraka (self-rule) Day
October 20	Kenyatta Day
December 12	Uhuru/Jamhuri (Independence/Republic) Day
December 25	Christmas Day
December 26	Boxing Day

Movable Dates:
Good Friday, Easter Monday, Idd-ul-Fitr

R **RADIO and TV.** Kenya has one English-language radio station that can be picked up throughout the country. The station broadcasts from 6 a.m. to 11.10 p.m. You can tune in to international news at 7 a.m., 9 a.m., 1 p.m., 5 p.m., 7 p.m. and 9 p.m. International news summaries are broadcast every hour, on the hour. The Swahili station is strong on good local and international popular music.

On the coast, the Mombasa station adds some occasional local programming to the Nairobi broadcasts.

On Kenya's single TV channel, Swahili and English programmes come on the air at 5.30 p.m. and go off at about 11 p.m. Popular English-language features include international favourites and film series from Britain, Germany, the United States and Australia.

RELIGIOUS SERVICES. Christianity is the dominant religion of Kenya with adherents divided roughly equally among Roman Catholic, Protestant and Independent African faiths. There are also large communities of Moslems on the Coast and smaller communities in the north-eastern region, where people of Somali origin live. About one-third of the rural population still adheres to a variety of traditional religions. In the urban centres mosques and temples of various eastern faiths are much in evidence.

Nairobi is a major centre of the Independent African Church Movement. Every Sunday hundreds of groups gather on street corners, at bus stops, in parks and public halls for worship. Others march up and down the streets to the rhythm of drums in colourful clothes, carrying flags, singing and preaching. Some of the groups welcome guests, but most are suspicious of newcomers.

English services of the major Nairobi Catholic and Protestant congregations are announced in the daily newspapers on Saturdays.

church	**kanisa**
synagogue	**hekalu la kiyahudi**
mosque	**msikiti**
mass/the service	**sala ya misa/ibada**

SIGHTSEEING. Numerous tour operators offer excursions to points of interest in the major towns and cities, as well as to game parks and other sights. Hotel chains organize their own sightseeing tours en route from one hotel to another. Ask at a tourist office for a list of possible tours and firms.

You can with advance planning embark on a private photo safari, guided and protected by a professional armed hunter whose equipment and staff may include four-wheel-drive cars, five-ton lorries, trackers, gun-bearers, camp cooks and aides. The expedition can hardly be rushed, so plan on up to a week in the Kenyan bush. There is no doubt that this is the most exciting way of seeing the country, but the cost is prohibitive. Even a privately organized group safari is expensive and conditions are more cramped. Unfortunately, if you have to ask the price, the chances are you can't afford it.

TIME DIFFERENCES. The East African countries of Kenya, Uganda and Tanzania are on standard time, three hours ahead of GMT. It remains constant throughout the year (see chart on p. 124).

Sunrise and sunset times for major urban centres are published in the daily newspapers.

Winter Time chart:

New York	London	**Kenya**	Sydney	Auckland
4 a.m.	9 a.m.	**noon**	8 p.m.	10 p.m.

TIPPING. Tipping is often discouraged, but not forbidden in Kenya as it is in some of the African countries. So if you appreciate a service, tip at your discretion, but keep it moderate. Most good hotels and restaurants include a ten-percent service charge in the bill.

Is service included?   **Eti pamoja na utumishi?**

TOILETS (*choo,* pronounced "cho"). Ladies and Gentlemen are almost always indicated in English, accompanied by male and female symbols.

Wanawake (Ladies) and *Wanaume* (Gentlemen) appear in bold letters in public lavatories, and are generally warnings that the places ought to be avoided—unless in cases of extreme emergency. A 10-cent coin will open toilet doors in the public areas of hotels, but surprisingly, in the generally tourist-only areas, no charge is made.

TOURIST INFORMATION OFFICES. Bring your queries to the local tourist office, which will recommend the best shops, car hire firms and hotels and advise on tours, recreation and any other subject. A wide range of guide-books, maps and pamphlets are also available.

The Nairobi Bureau, operated by the Kenya Tourist Development Corporation, is centrally located near the Hilton Hotel:

P.O. Box 42278, tel. 23285/21855 (open from 8.30 a.m. to 12.30 p.m. and 2–5 p.m., Monday to Saturday).

Similar information is available on the coast at the Mombasa Information Bureau near the tusks on Moi Avenue (formerly Kilindini Road), tel. 25428 (open from 8 a.m. to noon and 2–4.30 p.m.).

Kenya Tourist Offices abroad:

United Kingdom: 13, New Burlington St., London W.1.

U.S.A.: 15 East 51st Street, New York, N.Y. 10022.
Doheny Plaza, Suite 111–112, 9100 Wilshire Boulevard, Beverly Hills, California 90212.

TRANSPORT

Buses: City buses operate in Nairobi and Mombasa and provide an excellent opportunity for seeing the city centres and suburbs at low rates. Visitors are advised to avoid peak hours, when the buses will be very crowded. The best times to use the city buses are from 9.30 a.m. to 12 noon and 2.30 to 4 p.m. Fares are paid on the bus to the conductor.

There are no route maps on the streets or at bus stops, as these change frequently. Maps of current routes are available at the tourist office and most hotels.

There are inter-city buses of a reasonable standard connecting Nairobi with all main centres and crowded country buses connecting villages to the latter. These local buses are not reliable nor recommended except in an emergency.

Taxis: There are four types of taxi in the major urban centres of Kenya: Kenatco-owned, Yellow band, private and long distance. None have meters. Whatever you do, establish the fare *before* getting into the taxi.

Kenatco taxis use Mercedes Benz 200 vehicles. They charge per kilometre and you can consult lists of approximate distances to prominent landmarks and places of interest posted in most good hotels. Check the authorized fare with their office at the airport or at hotel reception desks.

Yellow band taxis come under the control of the municipal councils. Visitors should always check with the information bureau about the approximate charge for a journey before boarding the vehicle.

Private taxis come under no particular control and the vehicles may not be properly insured. Charges for waiting time and extra passengers are negotiable.

In addition to these, there are long-distance Peugeot taxi services which are shared by passengers who book their destination in advance. Prices are quite reasonable, and the ride relatively comfortable. These operate only between the major urban centres and do not go off the paved roads.

Matatus: These local private taxis compete directly with the bus services. They are mostly built from the wrecks of old cars and are filled to overflowing. Their—usually—unlicenced drivers will have no insurance and are particularly accident-prone. To be avoided at all costs.

Trains*: Passenger service on Kenya's single railway line from Mombasa to Kisumu is a railway enthusiast's dream. Trains are clean, cheap

T and supplied with good restaurant cars and well-stocked bars. Going at the leisurely pace of 35 miles per hour, the overnight trains are timed to leave the major stations of Mombasa, Nairobi and Kisumu about sunset and to arrive at these stations just after sunrise, providing good opportunities for day-long visits to either Mombasa or Kisumu from Nairobi, or day-long stopovers or visits to Nairobi from either place. Two consecutive nights on the train can prove tiring, however, so allow for at least one night's stopover.

W **WATER.** Other than in Mombasa's hotels, Nairobi is practically the only town where the tap-water is 100 per cent safe for drinking. However, if you are in doubt, bottled water is always available in bars. Nearly all lodges keep filtered water in jars or thermos jugs beside the bed. That is a direct warning that water from the tap is not safe, even for brushing teeth.

WILDLIFE ORGANIZATIONS. Conservationists and wildlife enthusiasts visiting Kenya may want to get in touch with the following societies:

Mountain Club of Kenya, P.O. Box 45741, Nairobi.

Cave Exploration Group of East Africa, P.O. Box 47583, Nairobi.

Members of these two organizations meet on Tuesday evenings at the Mountain Club of Kenya Clubhouse, Wilson Airport, from 7.30 p.m. Clubhouse telephone: 501747.

Other societies of interest are:

Geological Club of Kenya, P.O. Box 44749 Nairobi (no telephone).

East African National History Society, P.O. Box 44486, Nairobi; tel. 20141.

East Africa Wildlife Society, Nairobi Hilton Hotel, P.O. Box 20110; tel. 27047.

Wildlife Clubs of Kenya, National Museum, P.O. Box 40658, Nairobi.

Geographical Society of Kenya, P.O. Box 41887, Nairobi.

Index

An asterisk (*) next to a page number indicates a map reference. For index to Practical Information, see p. 107.

088/510 RP

SAFARI ROUNDUP

☐ Oryx ☐ Impala ☐ Eland ☐ Gerenuk

☐ Thomson's Gazelle ☐ Wildebeest ☐ Bongo ☐ Buffalo

☐ Greater Kudu ☐ Sable Antelope ☐ Dik-Dik ☐ Coke's Hartebeest

☐ Lizard ☐ Gecko ☐ Boomslang ☐ Leopard Tortoise

☐ Butterfly ☐ Termite ☐ Safari Ant ☐ Centipede

☐ Nile Crocodile ☐ Bush Pig ☐ Giant Forest Hog ☐ Hippopotamus